Choices & Strongholds
— By Mary A. Bruno, Ph.D.

Choices & Strongholds

— By Mary A. Bruno, Ph.D.

Choices
&
Strongholds

—Two Companion Books in One!
(2021 Edition)
How to Make Godly Choices & Dare to Pull Down Strongholds!

— By Mary A. Bruno, Ph.D.

Mary A. Bruno, Ph.D.,

author, and ordained minister, serves with her husband, the Reverend Doctor Rocco Bruno. She is Co-founder and Vice President of Interdenominational Ministries International, and Co-founder/Vice-Chancellor of IMI Bible College and Seminary in Vista, California. She has earned a Ministerial Diploma from LIFE Bible College; a Master of Theology, and Doctor of Ministry Degree from School of Bible Theology (which also awarded her the Honorary Doctor of Divinity Degree). She earned her Doctor of Theology Degree, from IMI Bible College & Seminary, and Doctor of Philosophy Degree in Pastoral Christian Counseling from the Evangelical Theological Seminary.

Watch for her new books at www.amazon.com.
or email imibcs@aol.com.
Visit the website www.ministrylit.com

Speaking Engagements:

Email: imibcs@aol.com

Or write:

Dr. Mary A. Bruno

P.O. Box 2107, Vista, California 92085-2107 United States of America

Choices & Strongholds
—Two Companion Books in One!
How to Make Godly Choices & Dare to Pull Down Strongholds!

(2021 Edition)

This combined version is of two previously published books entitled: *How to Make Godly Choices*, and *Dare to Pull Down Strongholds!* by Mary A. Bruno, Ph.D.

Publication Date:

November 9, 2020.

Printed in the United States of America

Mary A. Bruno, Vista, California, November 2020

International Standard Book Number ISBN 9780997668124

BISAC Category: RELO12040
Nonfiction/Religion/Christian Life/Spiritual Warfare, and Education and Reference/Education /Counseling/General

Library of Congress Control Numbers: 2018911329 and 2018914791,

Mary A. Bruno, Vista, CA

COMBO-VCS-2021ED-172-7.5X9.25-170P-042521

Choices
&
Strongholds

—Two Companion Books in One!
How to Make Godly Choices & Dare to Pull Down Strongholds!
(2021 Edition)

By
Mary A. Bruno, Ph.D.

COMBO-VCS-2021ED-172-7.5X9.25-170P-042521

To the dedicated chaplains across this nation and around the world, and their faithful teams of tireless volunteers, who diligently teach, train, encourage, comfort, and edify those who are learning to rightly apply God's Word and reap His great blessings.

— By Mary A. Bruno, Ph.D.

Acknowledgments

This book is a combined and reformatted version of the two companion books entitled, *How to Make Godly Choices,* and *Dare to Pull Down Strongholds!,* authored by Mary A. Bruno, Ph.D.

To avoid confusion regarding for which book the front matter and back matters were written, the original *acknowledg*ments and other pages were left in place within Book One — *How to Make Godly Choices* and within *Book Two—Dare to Pull Down Strongholds!* Both books share one table of contents.

— By Mary A. Bruno, Ph.D.

Contents

Preface

Publishing two books, *How to Make Godly Choices,* and *Dare to Pull Down Strongholds!,* one day apart on December 19 and 20 in 2018, was a challenge and a relief rolled into one. Immediately after that, God led to donate copies of the books to jails, juvenile halls, recovery homes, and veterans.

March 8, 2019— An incarcerated man in his twenties wrote that he was in solitary confinement and "in a bad state of mind in thoughts and spirit." When he found a copy of *How to Make Godly Choices* on the book cart and started reading it, his life changed quickly. He asked for *Dare to Pull Down Strongholds*

May 10, 2019— A lady inmate/trustee wrote of how her life had changed while she was reading *How to Make Godly* Choices, at 3:45 a.m. Her heart and pencil overflowed with God's love and the newfound joy of her salvation.

December 15, 2019— A man wrote that he had just finished reading chapter two of the *"Choices"* book, and had filled out his "contract with God" (Gave his life to Christ.) He enclosed a beautiful sliver cross made from gum wrappers that were folded into shinny little squares and woven together. How precious!

December 19, 2019— Who but God? A lady's letter was postmarked on the first anniversary date of when *How to Make Godly Choices* was published. She wrote that she had memorized ALL OF THE 100 BIBLE MEMORY VERSES—from *How to Make Godly Choices.* And that, my friend, was God's glorious gift to this thankful author.

There was no indication when writing these books that God wanted them to be donated for our veterans, and for those who were incarcerated or in recovery. As you can see, the books were combined under one cover, so that each recipient may have both copies at once. This new format (with most of the blank pages removed) has helped to reduce production costs.

We donated about a thousand books during the first year of publication. Additional copies were requested for the San Diego County Detention Facilities in 2020. Other copies will be given to a veterans' organization, which, by God's grace and the help of His like-hearted servants, will also be donated in this new one-volume format.

> And Jesus looking upon *them* said to them, With men this is impossible; but with God all things are possible.
> —Matthew 19:26 ASV
> *American Standard Version*
> Public Domain

Mary A. Bruno. Ph.D.

— By Mary A. Bruno, Ph.D.

BOOK: ONE

How to Make Godly Choices

—*Tips for Terrific Results!*
(Updated 04/25/2021)
By
Mary A. Bruno, Ph.D.

V144-P-6.69x9.61/113 pt/122018-082319/17

Mary A. Bruno, Ph.D.,

author, and ordained minister, serves with her husband, the Reverend Doctor Rocco Bruno. She is Cofounder and Vice-President of Interdenominational Ministries International, and Co-founder/Vice-Chancellor of IMI Bible College and Seminary in Vista, California. She has earned a Ministerial Diploma from LIFE Bible College; a Master of Theology, and a Doctor of Ministry Degree from School of Bible Theology, (which also awarded her the Honorary Doctor of Divinity Degree). She earned a Doctor of Theology Degree from IMI Bible College & Seminary, and a Doctor of Philosophy Degree in Pastoral Christian Counseling from the Evangelical Theological Seminary.

Her talks include humor, witty insights, and Scripture. She has ministered in the USA and abroad. Turnouts skyrocketed when she presided over the Vista Women's Aglow. Her "Words in Season" radio broadcast aired in the 1980s and '90s over KPRZ and KCEO near San Diego.

Watch for Dr. Bruno's new books at www.amazon.com.
or email imibcs@aol.com

Speaking Engagements:
Email: imibcs@aol.com
Or write:
Dr. Mary A. Bruno
P.O. Box 2107
Vista, California 92085-2107
United States of America

Publication Date: December 19, 2018
Printed in the United States of America

Mary A. Bruno, Vista, California, December 2018

International Standard Book Number ISBN-13: 978-1729803400
International Standard Book Number ISBN-10: 1729803407

BISAC Category: RELO12040
Religion/ Christian Life/ Inspirational and Christian Education/General

Library of Congress Control Number: 2018911329

Mary A. Bruno, Vista, CA

To the zealous teens and adults, who want and are ready to learn how to think things thru and make godly choices that bring good results—before leaping into life-changing decisions with their unexpected, long-term results.

— By Mary A. Bruno, Ph.D.

Foreword

Many of us wonder where we would be if things had turned out differently. We think of our decisions, successes, or failures. We dreamed of what we would do and changes we have to endure. Would we go to college? What would we study? Who would we marry? What kind of person should we look for? How could we impact the world to make it a better place?

Some of these concerns may have come to pass. Who did we marry? Did it work out? What changes could I apply to make it better?

Am I studying what is needed for me to excel in my chosen field? Do I want to do this for the rest of my life? Am I doing the work that I expected? If not, why not? Is it too late to go back to school? Of course not! So why not move forward? What hinders you from fulfilling your dream? If you are in school, are you making the best grades that you can right now?

Do your friends encourage you to be all that you can be? If not, why waste time on them? You are priceless! You are worth having people around you who have a positive influence, make you happy, and encourage you in your work and education.

Dr. Mary A. Bruno has been a tremendous influence in my life. I enrolled in her Bible College because I was in ministry and wanted to excel. At 45 years of age, it was a bit scary; but, that was the best decision I could have made because it changed my whole life. It gave me the courage to dare to do what I loved most, which was to serve the LORD and His people. I am forever grateful for her encouragement, wisdom, and friendship.

One wise or foolish decision can change the entire direction of a person's life. Dr. Bruno's book should be included in the curriculum for every high school and college. Everyone, no matter what age, needs the wisdom that leaps from these pages. Now is a good time to hear from God and chart a new course for your life!

I pray that as you glean from the words of wisdom in this book, you will realize that "with God, all things are possible," because He has all of the right answers. As you follow His directions, you will enjoy the life you were meant to live! May God fill you with ongoing courage to boldly pursue all that is right and best for you. Go for it!

Rev. Dr. Barbara A. Yovino,
Associate Pastor at Gateway City Church, in Brooklyn, NY; New York State Coordinator for the Day to Pray for the Peace of Jerusalem; New York Director of God.tv Prayer Line; Advisor to IMI Bible College & Seminary, and Vice-Pres./ Director of the Christian Hope Network, in Brooklyn, NY. Prayer Line: 718-238-4600, www.chn.cc. Visit her and CHN on Facebook!

— By Mary A. Bruno, Ph.D.

Acknowledgments

Special appreciation belongs to God's generous people who have helped to make this book a reality, especially the Reverend Doctor Rocco Bruno, my tri-lingual husband, a man of God, and missionary to Italy.

Others who have shared editorial comments:

Pastor Geremia Albano, Senior Pastor, and his lovely wife, Michela, Chiesa Evangelica di Caposele, Avellino, Italy.

Ministers Ludovico Albano and Fiorella Merino, serving in the provinces of Naples, Salerno, and Avellino, in South Italy.[1]

Elizabeth Caputo, Board Member and Prayer Minister for Christian Hope Network (CHN), Brooklyn, NY.

Arnet McKinney-Crespo, Certified Temperament Counselor, Prayer Intercessor and Phone Prayer Minister for Christian Hope Network (CHN), Brooklyn, NY.

The Reverend Doctor Rosa L. Davis, Founder of The Gleaning Field, (homeless ministry) in Vista, CA,[2]

Mrs. Jacqueline S. Francis, Phone Prayer Minister, Christian Hope Network (CHN), Educator, Brooklyn, NY.

The Reverend Doctor, Deone Gushwa, God's dedicated servant, San Marcos, CA.

The Reverends, Bob, and Daralene Hardrick, President, and Secretary, Full Gospel Business Men's Fellowship International, San Diego–South Bay Chapter.

Michelle Hoefflin, Co-Pastor, The Hills Church, Arcadia, CA.

The Reverends, Duane and Amy Hoover, and daughter Christina, Vista CA.

Amy Stoehr, Co-Pastor, The River Family Church, 390 Mimosa Ave., Vista, CA.[3]

The Reverend, Mary Anne Moyer, B.C.Ed., Artist, designed the graphic that introduced each chapter, Vista. CA.

Pastor Shirley Matthews was among the first to "lean on me hard" to offer these tips in book form, St. Luis, MO.

Catherine Sepe, Office Manager, Prayer Minister, Brooklyn, NY.

The Reverend, Carrie Smith, Fallbrook, CA.

Denny Steficek, Prayer Minister, Campbell, NY.

The Reverend Barbara Anne Yovino, Ph.D., Vice-Pres./Dir. of the Christian Hope Network, Brooklyn, NY; Associate Pastor at Gateway City Church, Brooklyn; New York State Coordinator for the Day to Pray for the Peace of Jerusalem; New York Director of God.tv Prayer Line;

and Advisor to IMI Bible College & Seminary.

San Diego Christian Writers Guild (SDCWG), San Marcos Chapter hosted by Barbara Waite, with Sandy Anderson, Joni Doyle, Jan Flickinger, and Pat Whistler, gave tireless, valuable, and insightful suggestions and tips.

Other Writers—Blessings to the many gifted writers whose books and websites (listed in the bibliography) enhanced the research phase. Any errors or omissions were purely unintentional.

May God reward each person's labor for His glory.

Mary A. Bruno. Ph.D.

Preface

This book is for those who want or need to understand how to think things through and make godly and wise choices that will bring a lifetime of God's sweet peace and prosperity.

Have you or someone you know ever longed to undo a decision that ended badly, and wished to have another chance to do it right? As many have learned, we cannot unsay harsh words, undo crimes, undo what we did to our bodies, or unbreak God's laws and laws of the land.

Yes, God is merciful and will forgive our ignorant and willful failures and sins. Yet, as one's family, criminal record, social media, and the press will attest, memories of our good or bad choices may linger for a lifetime.

Wise folks may learn to weigh new opportunities with their possible results and make godly choices that grace life's path with God's timely blessings that yield sweet memories.

The reader may be starting out on his or her own or have lived long enough to know that being able to make wise choices is vital for a happy life. May the reader understand, apply these practical tips, and become better prepared to take giant leaps forward on God's wisdom path that leads to divine blessings, peace, joy, and great success.

Blessed is the man that walketh not in the counsel of the ungodly, nor standeth in the way of sinners, nor sitteth in the seat of the scornful.

But his delight is in the law of the LORD; and in his law doth he meditate day and night.

And he shall be like a tree planted by the rivers of water, that bringeth forth his fruit in his season; his leaf also shall not wither; and **whatsoever he doeth shall prosper**.

The ungodly are not so: but are like the chaff which the wind driveth away.

Therefore the ungodly shall not stand in the judgment, nor sinners in the congregation of the righteous.

For the LORD knoweth the way of the righteous: but the way of the ungodly shall perish.   —Psalm 1:1–6
King James Version (KJV)
Public Domain, Emphasis added

By God's grace, may you become like the godly person in Psalm One—planted, thriving, fruitful—and a fulfillment of God's promise that "Whatever he does (whatever *you* do) shall prosper."

Scripture Translations Used:
The New King James Version (NKJV) is the primary source of Scripture unless otherwise shown.

Scripture taken from the New King James Version. Copyright © 1982 by Thomas Nelson, Inc. Used by permission. All rights reserved.

Choices & Strongholds

— By Mary A. Bruno, Ph.D.

Other translations that were cited as used:

American Standard Version (ASV) Public Domain

The Amplified Bible. Scripture quotations marked (AMP) are taken from The Amplified Bible, Old Testament. Copyright © 1965, 1987 by Zondervan Corporation. Used by permission. All rights reserved. Scripture quotations marked (AMP) are also taken from The Amplified Bible, New Testament. Copyright © 1954, 1958, 1987, by The Lockman Foundation. Used by permission.

Jubilee Bible 2000 (JUB) Copyright © 2013, 2020 by Ransom Press International

The *King James Version* (KJV). Public Domain.

The Passion Translation (TPT). The Passion Translation®. Copyright © 2017 by BroadStreet Publishing® Group, LLC. Used by permission. All rights reserved. thePassionTranslation.com

---

[1] www.ludovicoalbano.com
[2] www.gleaningfield.com
[3] www.theriverfamilychurchnc.org

"Your word *is* a lamp to my feet
And a light to my path" (Psalm 119:105, (NKJV)).

1
Choices Are Required

From time to time, all of us will face difficult, and sometimes life-altering decisions as we struggle to weigh and sort our options. Life was simpler when we were children, and our parents or guardians ruled on critical matters. Yet, as we mature, we must do the praying, we must listen to good counsel, and then we must consider our choices, steer our course, and live with the results.

The responsibility for our choices rests solely upon us; the weight of which is often substantial. Therefore, we will study God's great counsel that becomes clearer as we diligently apply His Word. We will learn to choose wisely, walk uprightly, and enjoy His blessings, peace, and prosperity that top our highest hopes and expectations.

It would be nice if we could peek through time and see the outcomes of our various opportunities and choices. God has not granted us that ability, because He wants us to trust Him to lead, guide, and take care of us as we live by faith in His promises. This is why we must not visit fortune-tellers, consult the Ouija board, have our tea leaves read; seek direction from crystal ball gazers, tarot card readers, palm readers, or rely on horoscopes or witchcraft. Such activities are forbidden in Scripture. We must be faithful to God and not cheat on Him by committing spiritual adultery with false prophets.

Many, including myself (when I knew no better), have found out the hard way, after pursuing advice from the devil's counterfeit counselors, that dark shadowy spirits followed them, moved about in their homes, and filled their hearts with terror. When one relies on such ungodly counselors, he or she mistakenly allows demonic activity into his or her life and home—which will affect the whole family.

If this has happened to you, it is not too late. Ask God to forgive you, then reject and stop all interaction with the devil's prophets. In Jesus' name, command the dark spirits to leave you, your family, and your home. Jesus will back you up. God's counselors (pastors and teachers) will help you to apply His Word that

— By Mary A. Bruno, Ph.D.

will bring wisdom, drive out fear, and restore peace.

If we want to please God, we must study His Word, submit our plans for His approval, welcome His abiding presence, follow His lead, and rest assured that He will guide us. If we want His best in life, we must make God-approved decisions and then follow through. If invited, Jesus will walk with us and help us to make terrific choices.

Once, everyone in the human race (all two of them) walked closely with God. Then, when Adam and Eve (our representatives) either forgot or ignored God's instructions and relied on their limited and inexperienced judgment while in the Garden of Eden, they sinned and ruined things for all of us. God had to evict them because they had become stained with sin, and sin could not stay in His Holy Presence.

From then on, keeping peace with God required many sacrifices and attention to details. God gazed down from Heaven and could tell that His people wanted to do what was right, but they just couldn't seem to get the hang of it. Their stinky sins kept piling up.

> There is a way *that seems* right to a man,
> But its end *is* the way of death.
> —Proverbs 14:12 (NKJV)

Jesus offered to come to earth and rescue us. Father God still loves us dearly and wants all of us to live in His Kingdom. He knew for that to happen, we would need Jesus Christ— *The Redeemer.*

> Jesus said to him, "I am the way, the truth, and the life. No one comes to the Father except through Me."
> —John 14:6 (NKJV)

Jesus loved, and still loves, us enough to pay the price that freed us from sin's stain, control, and penalty. He left the beauty and majesty of His home in Heaven, where everyone adored Him and sang His praises. He came to earth, took on the role of a common laborer, and was either loved or despised by those who knew Him.

He overcame temptations and abstained from youthful lusts and sins that were common to young men. He healed the sick, restored those who were disfigured, healed blind eyes, and raised the dead. But Jesus's greatest miracle happened when He yielded Himself on the Cross, dismissed His Spirit, died, stormed Hell's corridors, and overthrew Satan's power, including death, rose again, and returned (alive) to Heaven.

Jesus—both God and man, is the only one to have broken none of God's laws (never sinned). This qualified Him to offer Himself as the Holy Sacrifice that takes away the sin of all who believe and receive

Choices & Strongholds

— By Mary A. Bruno, Ph.D.

Him. He took the penalty for every bad thing we ever did and ever will do, gave us a full pardon (deleted our records), and welcomes us into God's family, to be with Him forever.

Still, there is a crucial choice we must make before we can enjoy that provision. God wants us to, not only trust Him, but admit (say aloud) we have sinned, and say we *believe* Jesus Christ is God's only begotten Son (born of God's divine genes and DNA). He wants to hear us say we believe Jesus died for us and rose again, and we *receive* (welcome) Him as our personal LORD and Savior.

Before we can tell folks we have received Christ, it might be wise to speak with Him about it first. If you want to make this choice, you may do so today. Do not worry about not being good enough; none of us are. God is very kind about taking us imperfect folks in whatever condition He finds us. He cleans us up, He restores our souls, and He helps us to become more like Him.

We must not miss this critical point. What makes the whole thing work is a glorious change that happens the second anyone receives the LORD Jesus. He or she will instantly become a new person. God's Presence will live within him or her forever because he or she will have become part of His family.

> For God so loved the world that He gave His only begotten Son, that whoever believes in Him should not perish but have everlasting life. For God did not send His Son into the world to condemn the world, but that the world through Him might be saved. —John 3:16–17 (NKJV)

> Wherefore if any man is in Christ, *he is* a new creature: the old things are passed away; behold, they are become new. —2 Corinthians 5:17 (ASV)

> Behold, I stand at the door and knock: if any man hear my voice and open the door, I will come in to him, and will sup with him, and he with me. —Revelation 3:20 (ASV)

Before we can expect Jesus to be our counselor and helper, we need to receive Him and entrust ourselves entirely and *permanently* to Him—The Messiah—our One and Only LORD and Savior. If you have not already done so, you can have your God encounter today.

Jesus is waiting to welcome you into His family and is more interested in your heart's attitude than your choice of words. But, He does want to hear you admit you have sinned, ask His forgiveness, and say aloud that you believe He is God's only begotten Son, and you are receiving Him as your LORD and Savior.

The following true story about Rocco Bruno's encounter with Jesus was not in the first issue of this book, however; it seems fitting to include a portion of it here, to help readers understand *how important receiving Jesus is to God.*

Rocco Bruno, born and raised in Italy, had childhood encounters with Jesus, and did his best to honor God. He did not know the Lord had a divine appointment for him—in a faraway land. . .

At age twenty, Rocco boarded a boat going south-west to **Venezuela.** He, worked as a mechanic, learned to speak Spanish, and in 1961, returned to Italy, and opened a mechanic shop.

Mudslide/Canada

Two years later— *a landslide* buried his business under *30 feet of mud.* God was still working His plan, when Rocco traveled *west to Montreal, Ontario, Canada*, learned to speak French, and worked as a mechanic.

By 1966, he was ready for a week-long, train ride west to *Vancouver, British Columbia, Canada,* where he worked at his trade for four cold knee-aching years.

United States of America

In 1969—Rocco threw his bags, into the car and headed south down the I-5 Freeway, to Los Angeles, California in *the United States of America —with seventy-five-dollars ($75)* in his pocket.

He studied English, worked as a mechanic for a dealership, at three dollars ($3) an hour, and wished he could have his own business again.

God would use that for good.

> For promotion *comes* neither from the east, nor from the west, nor from the desert.
>
> But God *is* the judge; he puts down one and sets up another.
> —Psalm 75:6–7
> Jubilee Bible 2000 (JUB)

Application to Chevron

September1972—Knowing very little English, Rocco could barely complete the application for a Chevron Dealership. The interviewer said, nearly 100 applicants with lots of money wanted *that station*—but *"For some reason,"* he was inclined to give it to him.

God must have nodded and smiled when Rocco became a Chevron Dealer for *that station* by Melrose and Fairfax in Los Angeles.

In Business Again

Rocco could not afford to hire employees. He worked *18 hours a day, seven-days-a-week*. The long work days and no time off, wore on his nerves. His frown deepened as he *screamed and cursed at people*, including customers. But, God's plan for Rocco was still in place.

Lady With Car Trouble

February 12, 1975— Moments after exiting the San Bernardino Freeway, the left front wheel fell off Mary's car— in front of Rocco's station.

He drove her to work, fixed her car, and asked her to go on a date with him. She, being a Christian, agreed—If they could go to church. (She thought "he had the personality of a clam" and needed God's joy of salvation.)

Divine Appointment

Near 1:00 AM, March 15, 1975— After another date with Mary (to a Christian meeting), Rocco was driving on the San Bernardino Freeway, about 20 miles from his Beverly Hills apartment, when. . .

Jesus Spoke to him on the Freeway!

Jesus said, "Rocco, you have known Me all of your life, but *you have never received Me."*

"Well, I'ma receiva Ya now," Rocco said with his heavy Italian accent.

In the instant Rocco said he *received Him*, Jesus came into his life and the smoking, screaming, cussing, Italian immigrant became a whole new creation in Christ.

> But as many as received him, to them gave he the right to become children of God, *even* to them that believe on his name:
> —John 1:12 (ASV)

Different

When they met for lunch the next day, Rocco was all bright-eyes, sweetness, and smiles—**Gushing** his new life in Christ!

"What happened to you?", Mary demanded. She had not seen him so alive or smiling like that before. *"You are so different! Did you get saved? Did you receive Jesus as your Savior?"*

Rocco grinned and told her all about his freeway encounter with Jesus.

> Wherefore if any man is in Christ, *he is* a new creature: the old things are passed away; behold, they are become new.
> —2 Corinthians 5:17 (ASV)

God's Love

Rocco suddenly **loved** everybody! Instead of screaming and swearing, praise songs welled up in his heart and flowed from his lips. People

— By Mary A. Bruno, Ph.D.

could see he was a changed man. (Rocco Bruno had become a new king and priest to God.)

Are You Sure?

If you, like Rocco and so many others, believe in Jesus, but are not sure if you have ever told Him, you *received Him* as your Savior, you may take care of that very important step right now.

The following prayer will help to confirm that you have *received* Jesus with His amazing joy and assurance of your salvation.

**Sample Prayer to Make
Sure You Have Received Jesus**

Dear Lord Jesus — **I want to tell You,**

I believe You are God's Son Who died on the Cross and rose again to free me from the stain and penalty of all my sins.

I confess that I have sinned, and **I receive You** as my Lord and Savior. Thank You for forgiving me, cleansing me, and making Your own.

You said, if I came, You would **receive me**.

Thank You for hearing my prayer, and welcoming me into God's family.

I also, **receive** Your Holy Spirit, and His power to help me to live a life that is pleasing to You.

I love You, Lord Jesus! Amen.

Name: _____

Date: _____Time:_____

After receiving the LORD, it is important to regularly attend a Bible teaching church, and to tell others you are serving God.

After believing and receiving Jesus (The Messiah), you will experience a joyful new connection with Him. You will stop feeling guilty about the wrong choices in your past because Jesus will have cleansed your soul and given you a *full pardon*! It will have happened while you were still praying!

> And it shall come to pass that, before they call, I will answer; and while they are yet speaking, I will hear.
> —Isaiah 65:24 (ASV)

That's right! Suddenly, because God is love and He lives within your heart, you will love everybody and want to be in Father God's house (church) every time the doors open. This is one of the signs that Jesus is in your life—He loves to be in His Father's house—and so will you.

Sinful expressions and habits will suddenly feel very inappropriate. This is not because of what you have done, but because of what the LORD Jesus Christ—Yeshua!—God's Messiah's Presence has done within you. He will live, reign, and set up housekeeping within your inner-most being.

Trust me; since He is going to be living there (within you), He will help

Choices & Strongholds

— By Mary A. Bruno, Ph.D.

you to keep the place (your life) clean and orderly.

New Position

Your new position with God will be, a child of the King of kings and His ambassador/representative.

> For you did not receive the spirit of bondage again to fear, but you received the Spirit of adoption by whom we cry out, "Abba, Father." The Spirit Himself bears witness with our spirit that we are children of God, and if children, then heirs— heirs of God and joint heirs with Christ, if indeed we suffer with *Him,* that we may also be glorified together.   —Romans 8:15–17 (NKJV)

> Now then, we are ambassadors for Christ, as though God were pleading through us: we implore *you* on Christ's behalf, be reconciled to God.
> —2 Corinthians 5:20 (NKJV)

Irrevocable

Your walk with Father God and familial relationship is just getting started. He will help you to develop as a member of His family, and as a king and priest to God. Yep! Imagine that! *You will be a king and a priest—to God.* That's right. Read it here.

> But you *are* a chosen generation, a royal priesthood, a holy nation, His own special people, that you may proclaim the praises of Him who called you out of darkness into His marvelous light;   —1 Peter 2:9 (NKJV)

> To Him who loved us and washed us from our sins in His own blood, and has made us kings and priests to His God and Father, to Him *be* glory and dominion forever and ever. Amen.
> —Revelation 1:5b–6 (NKJV)

> "And have made us kings and priests to our God;
> And we shall reign on the earth."
> —Revelation 5:10 (NKJV)

Obeying God's Word brings good results. However, acts of rebellion (a child's willful disobedience or when an adult defies a superior) can separate relationships.

> "For rebellion *is as* the sin of witchcraft,
> And stubbornness *is as* iniquity and idolatry.
> Because you have rejected the word of the LORD,
> He also has rejected you from b*eing* king."   —1 Samuel 15:23 (NKJV)

Note: One who worships (prays to) an idol, or prays to anything or anyone other than God, commits idolatry.

If you have rebelled against God, He is waiting for you to tell Him about it and receive forgiveness. He will cleanse, restore, and never mention it again. (How Amazing!)

Get Out and Stay Out

Just because a person was wallowing in the filth of sin when Jesus rescued him or her does not mean he or she should ever go back and do it again. Jesus is the Good Shepherd, and we are His *sheep*— not dogs or swine! His sheep follow Him on new honorable paths and stay off the old ones. Those who return to sin will have bitter regrets.

> For if, after they have escaped the defilements of the world through the knowledge of the Lord and Saviour Jesus Christ, they are again entangled therein and overcome, the last state is become worse with them than the first. For it were better for them not to have known the way of righteousness, than, after knowing it, to turn back from the holy commandment delivered unto them. It has happened unto them according to the true proverb, The dog turning to his own vomit again, and the sow that had washed to wallowing in the mire.
> —2 Peter 2:20–22 (ASV)

After Jesus comes into one's life, sin's pleasures and disappointing payoffs will be ruined forever.

Why?

Because the believer will be a new person in Christ—born again into God's family—the old life will not fit anymore. If a believer should happen to slip back for another taste of tainted sin, he or she will quickly realize the terrible mistake.

The devil will rush in to torment and humiliate the fallen one with memories of what he or she had, what was done, what was lost, how he or she failed God, and weigh the person down with depressing joy-sapping guilt.

You will be tested! Stay ready to yield to God and resist (boot out) the evil one.

> You prepare a table before me in the presence of my enemies;
> You anoint my head with oil;
> My cup runs over.
> Surely goodness and mercy shall follow me
> All the days of my life;
> And I will dwell in the house of the LORD Forever.
> —Psalm 23:5–6 (NKJV)

You will be tested more than once! Stay ready to overcome.

You will be rewarded! Every passed test brings a special blessing, reward, or promotion, from Father God. He will stay at your side through every trial and temptation (Yes, all of them.—Think about that!) and be ready to celebrate your triumph. Expect to receive a fresh anointing (Holy empowering and

— By Mary A. Bruno, Ph.D.

equipping from God) while dining and visiting with Jesus after each victory.

Sadly, those who have returned to wallow in spiritual filth and drink the nasty dregs of sin have deeply regretted it.

If you are wise, you will choose to yield to God and resist the devil, instead of resisting God and yielding to His enemy. The rewards for each decision are very different. The choice is yours.

Your New Freedom

In a healthy relationship with God, you will be freed from living under the old sinful nature's control. Sin may have once "yanked your chain" and pulled you here and there. But now you are free and a new person with a new and godly mind—that sides with God's point of view. That is why you will love what God loves, hate what God hates, and can ignore sin's tugs that have no more power over you.

If you, as a believer, slip and take God's name in vain, the Holy Spirit will instantly reveal that you have done something very wrong. If anything like that happens, quickly thank God for His correction, ask and receive His forgiveness, and trust Him to help you to never do it again. Your loving Heavenly Father will help you to make godly choices that will steer you around pitfalls.

> If we confess our sins, he is faithful and righteous to forgive us our sins, and to cleanse us from all unrighteousness. —1 John 1:9 (ASV)

> For if you live according to the flesh you will die; but if by the Spirit you put to death the deeds of the body, you will live. For as many as are led by the Spirit of God, these are sons of God. —Romans 8:13–14 (NKJV)

Your New Helper

The Holy Spirit leads us to our full potential in Christ. He fortifies us to overcome challenges and enemy tactics. "Receiving" is our choice. If we want God's best, we will aim our "inner receivers" toward Heaven and receive His great benefits.

> "But **you shall receive power** when the Holy Spirit has come upon you; and you shall be witnesses to Me in Jerusalem, and in all Judea and Samaria, and to the end of the earth." —Acts 1:8 (NKJV) Emphasis added

Note: The *power* in Acts 1:8, is the same (*dynamis*) power that flowed through Jesus in Luke 5:17, and in believers in Ephesians 3:20, 2 Timothy 1:7, and 3:5. Jesus gave *His* power to us so we could do God's will on earth.

> By this we know that we abide in Him, and He in us, because He has given us of His Spirit.
> —1 John 4:13 (NKJV)

You will want to obey God's commandments and rejoice because He is not only with you—but is in you.

You will have the mind of Christ so that you can think like Jesus!

> Have this mind in you, which was also in Christ Jesus: who, existing in the form of God, counted not the being on an equality with God a thing to be grasped, but emptied himself, taking the form of a servant, being made in the likeness of men;
> —Philippians 2:5–7 (ASV)

God's Word lights our path and leads to great joy and huge victories. It assures if we walk in the light (not stand still or turn back), Jesus's blood will keep on cleansing us (not just a one-time cleansing) from sin.

Why?

Because, Father God hates every sin, but loves every sinner.

Jesus, the Good Shepherd of our souls, knows how and where to find His wandering sheep and bring them back to the safety of His fold.

He knows a stray may fall and get dirty, bruised, and broken on a wayward path—but that filthy, fallen member of the flock is still *His sheep*. Jesus will lovingly track it down, pick it up, clean it up, fill it up, build it up, love it up, and hold it so close, that it will never want to leave His side.

> But if we walk in the light as He is in the light, we have fellowship with one another, and the blood of Jesus Christ His Son cleanses us from all sin.
> —1 John 1:7 (NKJV)

Comments:

_____

_____

_____

Father God's instructions and practical tips for peace, joy, and harmony are next.

* * *

"Your word *is* a lamp to my feet
And a light to my path" (Psalm 119:105 (NKJV)).

2

Tips for
Making Great Choices

In Psalm 38, David was the king who made some wise choices and some that were downright dreadful. Yet, while under the anointing of the Holy Spirit, he wrote some encouraging words about God. King David's psalms hold great promises for all of us mistake-makers and overcomers.

Now, as we learn to look to the LORD and lean on Him for guidance, we will examine our hearts, look for Christ's example, and look for God's exits and rewards.

> The LORD will perfect *that which* concerns me;
> —Psalm 138:8a (NKJV)

Psalm 138:8 is a powerful statement about God's protection. He will work in a believer's life and bring it into divine order and completion—when the believer decides to do things God's way. Yes, God will find a way to bring to a good finish and to maturity all that concerns those who rely on Him. He does this sort of thing often and seems to enjoy displaying His creativity through the likes of us.

Knowing that our choices of today will have long-term results that affect our tomorrows will remind us to plan accordingly. Please consider the most critical choices that you must make in the near future and keep them in mind while reading the rest of this book.

Look to God

Before committing to anyone or anything while merely relying on limited "Eden-like" savvy and unreliable emotions—one should consult the LORD! He has all wisdom and will be delighted when we ask Him to get involved and share His heavenly insights. Jesus enjoys teaching us folks how to identify the way that is best for us. (Note: The Heavenly Teacher may bring up some enlightening questions during the learning process.)

Father God put Psalm 32:8–9 in writing so we could savor and replay it throughout a lifetime. Without mentioning any names, some of us will realize why He added that line about "the horse or mule." Not that He would call anyone "mule-headed." But, if the verse fits — apply it.[4]

> I will instruct you and teach you in the way you should go;
> I will guide you with My eye.
> Do not be like the horse *or* like the mule,
> *Which* have no understanding,
> Which must be harnessed with bit and bridle,
> Else they will not come near you.
> —Psalm 32:8–9 (NKJV)

Jesus used that verse to rein me in when I finally got around to taking Him seriously. He even gave me a little tune to go with it, which shows how badly I needed to learn the lesson. Until then, He let me continue in willful sin. But, when I started to follow Him and behave like one of His own, He started treating me like one of His own, which included His godly correction as He kept an eye on me.

The following questions/tips should help to bring matters into focus as one prayerfully conquers the decision-making process for wise choices. This includes asking God for wisdom—before signing any rental agreement, lease, loan documents, contract, or making any other kind of commitment. (Don't expect God to bless an agreement that contains your lies.)

> But the cowardly, unbelieving, abominable, murderers, sexually immoral, sorcerers, idolaters, and **all liars** shall have their part in the lake which burns with fire and brimstone, which is the second death.
> — Revelation 21:8b (NKJV)
> Emphasis added

1. __True,__False:
I asked God to reveal His will regarding my choice(s).

2. __True, __False:
I asked Father God to lead me and give me a heart that is willing to keep on walking in His blessed paths of righteousness.

3. __True, __False:
I asked Father God to give me enough wisdom and courage to choose what is best and right.

4. __True,__False:
I have forgiven all who have offended or harmed me.

5. __True, __False:
I asked Father God if He wants me to be involved with this person, group, or matter.

6. __True, __False:
I asked Father God to reveal any hidden flaws, lies, or schemes of which I need to be aware.

7. __True, __False:
I asked God to show me if my emotions are running amok or surrendered to His will.

Look Within

> For the LORD God is a sun and shield: the LORD will give grace and glory: no good thing will he withhold from them that walk uprightly.
> —Psalm 84:11(KJV)

While learning to walk uprightly, God's children must learn to abstain from fleshly cravings and do things His way. His rewards for obedience are delightful, but persisting in defiance and self-will leads to disappointing outcomes.

1. __True, __False:

I will walk uprightly and get to enjoy God's mind-boggling rewards.

2. __True, __False:

I will continue in my self-will and sinful ways and suffer the results that will not be fun or pretty.

> And there you shall remember your ways and all your doings with which you were defiled; and you shall loathe yourselves in your own sight because of all the evils that you have committed. —Ezekiel 20:43 (NKJV)

God tucked an encouraging promise in Psalm 37:5 for those who will entrust their choices to Him. This includes matters of education, employment, ministry position, whether or not to date, to marry, associate with someone, or to buy a vehicle, a house, entertainment, and so on.

Please circle the two things that a reader should do, and then underline what God will do.

> Commit your way to the LORD,
> Trust also in Him,
> And He shall bring *it* to pass.
> —Psalm 37:5 (NKJV)

3.__True, __False:

I asked God to influence my upcoming decision.

4.__ True,__False:

I know what God's Word says about the opportunity I am considering.

5.__True, __False:

I have decided to ignore God's will for this matter and press on to have things my way.

6.__True. __False:

I believe this opportunity is from God.

7.__True, __False:

I will pursue and follow the advice of my parents, pastor, minister, etc., who walk closely with the LORD.

8. Do you think God is in favor of this? __Yes. __No.

__I would rather not know.

9. Are my feelings overriding my wisdom?

__Yes. __No. __Probably.

> I can of myself do nothing: as I hear, I judge: and my judgment is righteous; because I seek not mine own will, but the will of him that sent me. —John 5:30 (ASV)

10. Is my wisdom controlling my feelings?

__Yes. __No. __Probably.

11. Am I looking for a way around what God's Word says, or trying to wrongly apply it so I will not feel guilty for doing what He forbids?

__Yes. __No. __Probably.

12. If so, how do I think that will work out for me in the future?

___I will obey God and be just fine.

___My stubborn and willful rebellion against God will be as bad as the sin of witchcraft and will steal my peace, joy, and blessings.

God's Word, as mentioned previously, reminds us:

> "For rebellion *is as* the sin of witchcraft,
> And stubbornness *is as* iniquity and idolatry.
> Because you have rejected the word of the LORD,
> He also has rejected you from *being* king." —1 Samuel 15:23 (NKJV)

13. __True, __False:

My defiant acts will put me at risk for the enemy to trick or trap me into an even worse sin or situation that will have me running scared.

14. __True, __False:

I will choose wisely, enjoy God's blessings, and skip the guilt.

Look for Christ's Example

You will know when you have decided to follow Christ's example (of when He prayed about going to the Cross) because you will be able to pray: "Not my will, but Yours be done," —and mean it!

> He went a little farther and fell on His face, and prayed, saying, "O My Father, if it is possible, let this cup pass from Me; nevertheless, not as I will, but as You *will.*" Matthew 26:39 (NKJV)

When one sincerely acts according to God's will, sweet peace, tranquility, and joy will saturate his or her soul. The believer will walk in victory, enjoy great success, and avoid years of fear, heartache, and grief from lasting damage done to oneself and others.

> For a righteous *man* may fall seven times
> And rise again,
> But the wicked shall fall by calamity. —Proverbs 24:16 (NKJV)

> The steps of a *good* man are
> ordered by the LORD,
> And He delights in his way.
> —Psalm 37:23 (NKJV)

If a struggling believer, who just cannot seem to get it right, stumbles and falls six times plus one, the LORD will still help that one back[5] up (again), dust him or her off (again), and declare him or her righteous (again). And that, my friend, is called "Blessed Assurance" and "Justification by Faith," which means—just as if we had never sinned.

Coach Jesus

After an under-achieving summer of walking out bad choices, I returned for the Fall semester at LIFE Bible College in Los Angeles. Feeling very unworthy, I knelt in the chapel, apologized to God, and said I did not know how to quit (school).

Suddenly, Coach Jesus came close by my side. In the vision, I had fallen while pushing an old-fashioned push plow with long wooden handles attached to a big spoked front wheel, with large curved prongs behind that broke up the ground. I was face down in the dirt with both hands holding on to the plow.

Jesus was suddenly at my side. He did not touch me or pick me up, but leaned over and coached me on how to get back up (again).

"Keep your hands on the plow, He said."

I hung on tighter.

"Now, pull one leg under you."

I pulled the right leg up.

"Pull the other leg up and get on your knees."

I obeyed again, feeling staggering weak.

"Now, pull one foot up under your knee."

I half-drug and half-pulled it up.

"Now pull the other foot up; then stand up and lean into the plow. The plow will support you."

I leaned into the plow, staggered forward, and continued to push through the hard ground.

The following verse became my "life preserver" while learning to serve God with my whole heart.

> Make me to go in the path of thy
> commandments;
> For therein do I delight.
> —Psalm 119:35 (NKJV)

Giving God permission to make us do what pleases Him opens a whole new avenue for Him to come closer with His trusty motivators. He will never force His will on anyone. But, when we step up and ask Him to motivate and help us to do what is best—which happens to be an exercise of our will, He will be happy to give us better desires with superior results.

As they say, "You can lead a horse to water, but can't make him drink—but, you can salt his oats!"

Father God may motivate us with a "sweet taste of honey," or if needed, a swarm of hornets or wailing police sirens. He will bring sufficient incentive for making excellent choices. He is very creative and has lots of exciting motivational tools. One of His favorite surprises is showing up and flooding one's soul with unspeakable joy that is full of glory. What a glorious way to be led of the LORD! Bless Him!

Great peace and happiness over-flow when we are in Father God's perfect will. He has some fantastic plans in the works for you. See, He even put it in writing. Don't you just love the way He has scheduled good things for *your* good future!

> For I know the thoughts that I think toward you, saith the LORD, thoughts of peace, and not of evil, to give you an expected end. —Jeremiah 29:11 (KJV)

1. Do you have peace about what-ever it is that you are considering?

__Yes. __No. __Sometimes.

2. What does God say about your involvement with or in this?

__Go for it! ___Wait. __No.

Train yourself to put the emotions on hold while thinking things through at the beginning of a matter, instead of jumping in during an emotional frenzy, and then later, trying to clean up the damage from a hasty and unwise choice.

Look Ahead to Your Reward

1. Will doing this cause you to rejoice and jump for joy with a clean heart and bright eyes before your loving LORD?

__Yes. __No. __Not sure.

2. Will Jesus smile, approve of the beautiful job you did, and call you His good and faithful servant?

__Yes. __No. __Maybe.

> But without faith *it is* impossible to please *Him,* for he who comes to God must believe that He is, and *that* He is a rewarder of those who diligently seek Him.   —Hebrews 11:6 (NKJV)

Reward?
  What reward?
  Take a good look at these reliable promises.

> The wicked *man* does deceptive work, But he who sows righteousness *will have* a sure reward.
>   —Proverbs 11:18 (NKJV)

> He who despises the word will be destroyed,
> But he who fears the commandment will be rewarded.
>   —Proverbs 13:13 (NKJV)

1. Will Jesus appreciate what you have done and give you a promotion in His Kingdom?

__Yes. __No. __I doubt it.

2. Will the results of your choice, be as gold tried in the fire (or as "wood, hay, and stubble" that will be consumed by fire)?

__They will be as gold tried by fire.

__They will be as wood, hay, and stubble.

__They will be as thistles in the wind that sow terrible seed.

Look at Your Christian Walk

Consider the possible outcomes of your plans.

1. How will this choice affect your spiritual life?

__It will enable me to help others to know how to receive Jesus.

__It will make me ashamed.

__Father God will be delighted over my decision.

2. How could this decision affect others who know about your walk with God?

__It will bring them grief.

__They will rejoice with me.

3. Does this look like an opportunity from God or an evil scheme from the enemy?

__A blessed opportunity from God.

__A sneaky trick, trap, or set up from the evil one.

Look for Exits

Look for God's escape ramps. He will make a way of escape with every temptation. Take it easy. Going too fast to turn around or take an exit could end in disaster.

> No temptation has overtaken you except such as is common to man; but God *is* faithful, who will not allow you to be tempted beyond what you are able, but with the temptation will also make the way of escape, that you may be able to bear *it.*
> —1 Corinthians 10:13 (NKJV)

1. When God made a way of escape from a trap or temptation, did you see it and run through it in time?

__Yes. __No. __Almost.

2. How do you feel about your "escape" choice(s)?

__Fantastic! __Not so good.

A teenager or young adult may not have lived long enough to know that one's actions of today do not just happen and disappear. They will replay in one's mind again and again over a lifetime.

Memories of our good deeds will bring smiles, but the "accuser of the brethren" will harass and torment us with mental replays of our failures long after we are old and grayed. A wise person will take God's exits—and get out—before things go wrong.

Double-mindedness

> If any of you lacks wisdom, let him ask of God, who gives to all liberally and without reproach, and it will be given to him. But let him ask in faith, with no doubting, for he who doubts is like a wave of the sea driven and tossed by the wind. For let not that man suppose that he will receive anything from the Lord; *he is* a double-minded man, unstable in all his ways. —James 1:5–8 (NKJV)

Since nobody brought it up, we should probably discuss double-mindedness.

"Double-what?"

It means:

Wavering, uncertain, doubting, divided in interest, two-spirited, vacillating in opinion or purpose, divided in interest namely, between God and the world.[6]

As God's Word explains, a double-minded (spiritually wobbly) person makes commitments but does keep them. He or she will be for something or someone on one day, but not the next. That kind of mindset could be brutal in relationships with God and others. Who can build anything long-term with an indecisive and wavering person?

One cannot walk in two different directions at once. Reliable people choose and follow through.

God forbid that you, dear reader, might ever make a life-long commitment to a double-minded person who cannot do the same. It would break your heart for him or her to make vows to you on your wedding day, and then embrace someone else soon after! Sadly, this kind of mentality is not unusual. This is another reason why a couple should date for at least a year before getting married, to allow time for unseen character traits to surface, which takes time.

One might wonder how Father God must feel when we act lovingly to Him on Sunday, but embrace worldly pleasures for the rest of the week. If we ask Him, He will teach us to overcome double-mindedness and honor our vows.

Next, we shall learn to recognize some of the sources and motivations behind opportunities.

Comments:

_____

_____

* * *

---

[4] Cnn.com - Transcripts, http://transcripts.cnn.com/TRANSCRIPTS/0906/13/i_if.0 1.html (accessed July 29, 2018).

[5] Contemplative Homeschoolno Lasting City, http://contemplativehomeschool.com/2017/09/08/no-lasting-city/ (accessed July 30, 2018).

[6] "G1374 - dipsychos - Strong's Greek Lexicon (KJV)." Blue Letter Bible. Accessed 26 Nov, 2018. https://www.blueletterbible.org//lang/Lexicon/Lexicon.cfm?Strongs=G1374&t=KJV

Choices & Stronghholds

— By Mary A. Bruno, Ph.D.

"Your word *is* a lamp to my feet
And a light to my path" (Psalm 119:105, NKJV).

3
Consider the Source

Have you noticed ideas may flood your mind while making essential choices? They may tend to glorify God, or yourself, or something or someone else. Humans tend to crave recognition, affirmation, and appreciation. The desires are not wrong in themselves, but excessive longing for them may become fertile soil for the enemy's wiles.

> Blessed *is* the man who endures temptation; for when he has been approved, he will receive the crown of life which the Lord has promised to those who love Him. Let no one say when he is tempted, "I am tempted by God"; for God cannot be tempted by evil, nor does He Himself tempt anyone. But each one is tempted when he is drawn away by his own desires and enticed.
> —James 1:12–14 (NKJV)

> But thou, O LORD, art a shield for me; my glory, and the lifter up of mine head. —Psalm 3:3 (KJV)

Father God will lovingly place His hand under your chin, look sweetly into your eyes, and gently lift up your head so that you can wear your crown of righteousness.

The enemy will entice you to violate God's protective laws, as in the account of Adam and Eve in the Garden of Eden. In the following passage, notice that God took them straight to the Garden of Eden—to the place where they would be tested. He took them to work in the garden where they could see the tree of the knowledge of good and evil, and explicitly told them not to eat of its fruit—because their act of disobedience—eating fruit from that tree—would kill them!

Father God was not trying to keep them from having fun. He was trying to save their lives—because He knew they would die spiritually on the day they disobeyed by eating that fruit. They were fully informed and fully free to choose to obey and live or disobey and die.

> Then the LORD God took the man and put him in the garden of Eden to tend and keep it. And the LORD God commanded the man, saying, "Of every tree of the garden you may freely eat;" —Genesis 2:15–16 (NKJV)

— By Mary A. Bruno, Ph.D.

> "But of the tree of the knowledge of good and evil you shall not eat, for in the day that you eat of it you shall surely die."
> —Genesis 2:17 (NKJV)

God's One Commandment came with a death warning for disobedience. This was not because He wanted to punish or kill Adam and Eve, but because their disobedient act, of eating of the fruit from that tree, would be deadly.

The new humans knew nothing about tests. God kindly gave them a pre-test-prep (Eating fruit from that tree would cause their death. They must not partake of it.) Not even one bite. Everybody understood the warning.

The lesson was similar to teaching people about having unprotected sex, which causes unwanted pregnancies and painful, deadly sexually spread diseases, or that using addictive substances, such as tobacco or feel-good drugs, causes addiction to them. Folks hear the warnings, but in moments of intense passion, they choose to bypass caution and take the risk.

They foolishly hope the predicted and proven results will not happen to them and are horrified when painful genital rashes, bumps, or open sores appear, a pregnancy test is positive, a fatal virus or disease attacks them, or the feel-good drug

they thought they could control—is in control of them.

As with Adam and Eve, unwise and deceived people may learn too late that one time was enough, and the deadly results are permanent.

Satan, Heaven's former angelic and talented worship leader, also learned about sin the hard way. Maybe that is why he still attacks worship leaders and teams. He must want his old job back, not to glorify God, but to worm his way into churches to steal attention and divert the glory from God to himself by showing off his musical skills and vocal abilities in the darkness rather than light.

> So the great dragon was cast out, that serpent of old, called the Devil and Satan, who deceives the whole world; he was cast to the earth, and his angels were cast out with him.
> —Revelation 12:9 (NKJV)

Seething with jealousy and wounded pride, the evicted fallen angel disguised as a serpent (before serpents were cursed and scary) wanted to get even with God. But how? The slick and sly smooth-talker knew he could not force Adam and Eve to sin. However, there had to be a way. He could lie and *entice* them to sin! Yes! That might work.

Scratching his smooth-talking head, the serpent squinted his flirty eyes and tried to think of a way to coax the couple to disobey God's instructions, which of course, would bring sin, death, and separation from God. He wondered how he could lure them into doing such a sinful thing. What kind of trick or lie might work on them? (And what kind of falsehood, flattery, scheme, or bait, might work or has worked on you?)

> Pride *goes* before destruction,
> And a haughty spirit before a fall.
> —Proverbs 16:18 (NKJV)

The fallen angel turned devil learned when God hurled him hard from heaven that pride leads to ruin. The schemer's freefall dropped him to earth like a rotten apple. His haughty and puffed-up spirit brought on his horrendous downfall. Hmmm... (He thought...) *Ah, ha!* He might be able to use Adam and Eve's pride to bring them down too. It was worth a try.

The devious defiler devised a deceitful scheme that would defy God's warning. The subtle sweet-talker sowed seeds of suspicion that stirred emotions and led the susceptible First Couple to doubt the outcome of what God said would happen. [The evil one's bait was working.] God's warning and statement of truth must have slipped their minds while they entertained the cunning serpent that twisted God's truth and spun an enticing web of deceit that stroked egos and awakened pride.

The serpent's conniving eyes darted about as he, the father of *all* liars, lured the innocent ones and urged them to act on his insinuations instead of embracing God's Word. He even implied God wanted to keep the "good stuff—becoming as gods" from them.

1. Has anyone ever enticed you to do what God forbids, and used "being in love," or "having a good time," or "being smart" or "easy money" as an excuse to sin?

__Yes. __No. __Possibly.

2. Did you resist, or fall for the lie?

__I resisted sin and yielded to God

__I resisted God and yielded to sin.

The tempter assured Adam and Eve they would be as gods. Becoming as gods sounded great! It was no surprise that the trickster still uses that same old lie today. It has worked quite well since Eden.

Please underline or use a highlighter to mark the serpent's disturbing question and lie in the following passages:

> Now the serpent was more cunning than any beast of the field which the LORD God had made. And he said to the woman, "Has God indeed said, 'You shall not eat of every tree of the garden'?"
> —Genesis 3:1 (NKJV)

Choices & Strongholds

— By Mary A. Bruno, Ph.D.

> And the woman said to the serpent, "We may eat the fruit of the trees of the garden; But of the fruit of the tree which *is* in the midst of the garden, God has said, 'You shall not eat it, nor shall you touch it, lest you die.'"
>
> Then the serpent said to the woman, "You will not surely die."
>
> "For God knows that in the day you eat of it your eyes will be opened, and you will be like God, knowing good and evil." —Genesis 3:2–5 (NKJV)

As indicated above, the evil one entices, but cannot force believers to disobey God. God's perfect will for us, is that our choices will be based—not on the world's view—but on God's statement of what is right, wrong, or acceptable. We get to use our renewed minds to prove and choose that which is God's good and perfect will.

Please, use a highlighter to emphasize the action words or phrases in Romans 12:1–2 that are most meaningful to you. Doing so will help you to retain the message. Then underline or draw a circle or square around each action that God probably wants you to take.

> I beseech you therefore, brethren, by the mercies of God, to present your bodies a living sacrifice,
> holy, acceptable to God, *which is* your spiritual service.
>   —Romans 12:1 (ASV)

> And do not be conformed to this world, but be transformed by the renewing of your mind, that you may prove what *is* that good and acceptable and perfect will of God.
>   —Romans 12:2 (NKJV)

Father God wants us to live in peace with others, keep busy, help others, be patient, kind and not vengeful, be happy, pray about everything, and give thanks to Him, no matter what happens. (Paraphrased from 1 Thessalonians 5:12-18).

Please circle or highlight words in the following passage that are most meaningful to you.

> And we urge you, brethren, to recognize those who labor among you, and are over you in the Lord and admonish you, and to esteem them very highly in love for their work's sake. Be at peace among yourselves.
> Now we exhort you, brethren, warn those who are unruly, comfort the fainthearted, uphold the weak, be patient with all.
>
> See that no one renders evil for evil to anyone, but always pursue what is good both for yourselves and for all. Rejoice always, pray without ceasing, in everything give thanks; for this is the will of God in Christ Jesus for you.
>   —1 Thessalonians 5:11–18 (NKJV)

Consider the Starting Point

Think about how an idea got started and those whom it will benefit.

1. Did this idea or suggestion come from someone living a godly life?

   __Yes.   __No.

2. Ask yourself, "Is this God's idea?"

   __Yes. __No. __Maybe.

3. Ask yourself, "Did this idea come from a friend or a fiend?"

   __Friend. __Fiend.

To be tempted is not a sin. Tests come to prove the good work that God has done in a believer's life and to prove he or she is an overcomer. Apparently, "overcomers" need something to overcome. This may be why we have so many tests and trials as we continue to mature and develop in Christ.

Tests are, likely, God's way of measuring and documenting our spiritual growth and progress; therefore, each new time of testing may come because we have achieved or overcome something and have climbed one step higher in Christ. It may also mean, in addition to advancing one step higher, that God wants to prove someone (probably you) is ready for another promotion in His kingdom.

> A wise *man* fears and departs from evil,
> But a fool rages and is self-confident.
> —Proverbs 14:16 (NKJV)

The wise person will "fear" [reverence God] and turn away from evil—not just once but will make a habit of godly and smart choices, honor Father God, and stay out of spiritual trouble. He or she will rush to change the channel when something weird, vulgar, or sinful comes on the TV screen.

An arrogant fool, on the other hand, shoots off his or her mouth; indulges in festive sin, thinks he or she can handle something (even though it got the best of him or her too many times before); and races blindly back down a one-way path to costly long-term trouble.

Strength Test

A lumberjack explained how a board's strength is tested and proven. The ends of the board are placed on top of two sawhorses that are spread apart the exact distance of the board's length. Weights are placed on the middle of the board. More weights are piled on until the board is so weighed down that it is close to, but never at or past, its breaking point.

The number of pounds or ounces the board can bear determines its strength and classification. The board's endurance level proves its strength, and fitness for popsicle sticks, backyard lattice, furniture, flooring, or for a humongous beam that can bear the massive weight of a cathedral's roof.

Choices & Strongholds

— By Mary A. Bruno, Ph.D.

> Beloved, do not think it strange concerning the fiery trial which is to try you, as though some strange thing happened to you; but rejoice to the extent that you partake of Christ's sufferings, that when His glory is revealed, you may also be glad with exceeding joy.
>
> —1 Peter 4:12–13 (NKJV)

Blessings, restoration, and a fresh new robe await all who finish their race.

> He who overcomes shall be clothed in white garments, and I will not blot out his name from the Book of Life; but I will confess his name before My Father and before His angels.
>
> —Revelation 3:5 (NKJV)

Imagine for a second what it would be like to stand before Father God's Throne in Heaven with King Jesus seated at His side.

A heavenly host of angels stands at attention by all of God's Redeemed. Suddenly Jesus looks you in the eye, beckons you with His finger to stand by Him, and says to everyone, "I would like you to meet (your name). He or she has belonged to me since (The date you *received* Him as your Savior.)

We have come through many hard trials and tests together, and now, here he or she is wearing a white robe and crown and is ready to rule and reign with Us. Just for fun (your name), since we have all eternity to do this, would you mind reciting all of those Bible verses (My Word) that you memorized while on Earth? We would all love to hear them, wouldn't we?"

Roaring cheers, shouts, shofar blasts, and clapping breaks forth from the angels and the Redeemed as you break into a grin, stand tall, raise your voice, and beginning with Psalm One, quote (with feeling) every single Bible verse that you have memorized.

About half-way through your recital, Jesus serves Heaven's version of pizza, as you keep right on quoting (with special emphasis and understanding), pausing from time to time to raise both hands and give Jesus a Heavenly High Five (shout "Hallelujah!" five times), with countless thousands of thousands joining in, until you have recited your very last verse.

Next, we shall inspect some spiritual fruit, the works of the flesh, and matters of legality.

Comments:

_____
_____
_____
_____
_____
_____

✳ ✳ ✳

"Your word *is* a lamp to my feet
And a light to my path" (Psalm 119:105 (NKJV)).

4

Take an Inspection

When making important decisions, a wise person may wait for the excitement and emotions to calm down. Choices charged with heated emotions could prompt impulsive decisions that might replay in one's mind and keep one awake at night. By now, you may have learned to recognize who or what might be urging your next move.

Occasionally, we may forget that God's defeated enemy is still in a rejection rage. Be not deceived, dear one; no matter how much he tries to sweet-talk you into following his lead instead of obeying God, the devil does not like you and is not your friend.

Sadly, I knew of a young man in his twenties who did not recognize or refuse ungodly counsel.

The man and his fiancée, whom we shall call Juan and Blanca (not their real names), were returning from his father's funeral. Juan parked the car in front of his friends' house, in San Marcos, California, as he had done so many times before, and said, "Wait for me, Honey. I'll just be a minute."

Sweet Blanca smiled, nodded, and stayed in the car.

Juan's street-wise pals were all set and waiting. They grinned a greeting, patted him on his shoulder, marched him straight to a back room, sat him down on the edge of the bed, rolled up his sleeve, wrapped a soft, tan-colored rubber hose around his arm, and shot-up their grieving friend with "a little something to help him feel better."

In the car, Blanca waited and watched fluffy silver/white cloud formations drift across the blue California sky. The minutes ticked by; five minutes, ten minutes, fifteen minutes. . . What could be taking him so long?

The drug was too strong! Juan passed out! His friends slapped his face and shook him, but could not wake him. Desperate, they injected him with a different drug to counteract the first one. They tried CPR. It didn't work! It was too late!

Juan died—in the house of his friends—about an hour after he

— By Mary A. Bruno, Ph.D.

buried his father—while Blanca, his trusting fiancée, waited in the car.

> There is a way *that seems* right to a man,
> But its end *is* the way of death.
> —Proverbs 14:12 (NKJV)

> Blessed *is* the man
> Who walks not in the counsel of
> the ungodly,
> Nor stands in the path of sinners,
> Nor sits in the seat of the scornful;
> But his delight *is* in the law of
> the LORD,
> And in His law he meditates day
> and night.
> He shall be like a tree
> Planted by the rivers of water,
> That brings forth its fruit in its season,
> Whose leaf also shall not wither;
> And whatever he does shall prosper.
>
> The ungodly *are* not so,
> But *are* like the chaff which the wind
> drives away.
> Therefore the ungodly shall not stand
> in the judgment,
> Nor sinners in the congregation of
> the righteous.
> For the LORD knows the way of the
> righteous,
> But the way of the ungodly shall
> perish.   —Psalm 1:1–6 (NKJV)

Inspect the Fruit/Flesh/Legality

Check the fruit, flesh, and legality (FFL) of those involved in a decision, including companies. Try to see if they reflect the Holy Spirit's influence, and which ones honor or break God's Laws and laws of the land. Rightly applying your findings with godly wisdom will lead you to make better choices with more pleasing and fruitful outcomes.

> I say then: Walk in the Spirit, and you shall not fulfill the lust of the flesh....
>
> Now the works of the flesh are evident, which are: adultery, fornication, uncleanness, lewdness, idolatry, sorcery, hatred, contentions, jealousies, outbursts of wrath, selfish ambitions, dissentions, heresies, envy, murders, drunkenness, revelries, and the like; of which I tell you beforehand, just as I also told *you* in time past, that those who practice such things will not inherit the kingdom of God.
> But the fruit of the Spirit is love, joy, peace, longsuffering, kindness, goodness, faithfulness, gentleness, self-control. Against such there is no law. And those *who are* Christ's have crucified the flesh with its passions and desires.
> If we live in the Spirit, let us also walk in the Spirit.   —Galatians 5:16, 19–25 (NKJV)

Note: *"Revellings"* from Galatians 5:21 (KJV), is defined as:

> "A nocturnal and riotous procession of half drunken and frolicsome fellows who after supper parade through the streets with torches and music in honour of Bacchus or some other. . ."

Choices & Strongholds

— By Mary A. Bruno, Ph.D.

"... deity, and sing and play before houses of male and female friends; hence used generally of feasts and drinking parties that are protracted till late at night and indulge in revelry."

[From: "G2970 - kōmos - Strong's Greek Lexicon (KJV)." Blue Letter Bible. https://www.blueletterbible.org//lang/lexicon/lexicon.cfm?Strongs=G2970&t=KJV]

1. __True, __False:

I believe Father God wants me to connect with these people or with the group that I have been considering.

2. __True, __False:

I think my Heavenly Father wants me to not be involved with this person/people/group.

Fruit

Review the spiritual fruit in Galatians 5:22–23. Then, answer the following questions to find if God's spiritual fruit is found in those involved in your decision. You may check more than one answer for the following sections in this chapter.

1. Love is evident in:

__me. __the other(s).

2. Peace and joy abound in:

__me. __the other(s).

3. Long-Suffering (patience) is evident in:

__me. __ the other(s).

4. Gentleness is at work in:

__me. __the other(s).

5. Goodness is obvious in:

__me. __the other(s).

6. Faith is active in:

__me. __the other(s).

7. Meekness is seen in:

__me. __the other(s).

8. Temperance (self-control) (being neither too hot nor too cold) is operative in:

__me. __ the other(s).

Comments:

_____
_____
_____
_____

Flesh

Circle works of the flesh in the following verses that are evident in those, including yourself, who are involved in your decision.

Adultery, fornication, uncleanness, lewdness, idolatry, sorcery, hatred, contentions, jealousies, outbursts of wrath, selfish ambitions, dissensions, heresies, envy, murders, drunkenness, revelries, and the like; of which I tell you, . . . that those who practice such things will not inherit the kingdom of God.   —Galatians 5:19b–21 (NKJV)

The good news is that a believer's fleshly works will lessen as he or she learns to conquer carnal desires and yield to God. (Prepare yourself for a possible surprise.) The *works of the flesh* are not from the devil—but are found *within us.* (Gasp!)

Thank God for His mercy, grace, and Holy Spirit power that strengthens us to be victorious overcomers in His kingdom.

Sadly, those who reject Jesus Christ must try to deal with and overcome them in their own strength.

1. Adultery or fornication: (sexual intercourse between unmarried persons, porn) is active in:

__me. __ the other(s).

2. Uncleanness (being morally impure, spiritually contagious, and unfit for good use) is present in:

__me. __the other(s).

3. Lasciviousness (wantonness, lacking moral or sexual restraint, lewd or lustful acts) are at work in:

__me. __ the other(s).

4. Idolatry (worship of or praying to someone or something other than the Living God) is practiced by:

__me. __ the other(s).

5. Witchcraft (involvement in sorcery or magic, including the misuse of legal or illegal drugs) is practiced by:

__me. __the other(s).

6. Hatred (prejudice or hostility) is evident in:

__me. __the other(s).

7. Variance (being disagreeable)[7] is visible in:

__me. __ the other(s).

8. Emulations[8] (ambition, to imitate, equal, or excel another) are at work in:

__me. __the other(s).

9. Wrath (heated vengeful anger or giving in to feelings of malice) is evident in:

__me. __ the other(s).

10. Strife (bitter conflict, violence, or the struggle for superiority) is apparent in:

__me. __ the other(s).

11. Drunkenness is seen in:

__me. __the other(s).

12. Seditions (coming against those in authority, or inciting others to rise up against lawful authority) are operative in:

__me. __the other(s).

13. Heresies (opinions contrary to the truth) are evident in:

__me. __the other(s).

14. Envying (resenting the possession or advantage enjoyed by another and craving to experience the same) is present in:

__me. __ the other(s).

15. Murders (murderous thoughts, encouraging or planning to have an abortion, or wishing someone dead) are at work in:

__me. __the other(s).

16. Revellings (wild parties) are practiced by:

__me. __ the other(s).

Legality

Consider God's laws and laws of the land for each of the following choices.

1. Could your choice open a way for physical or spiritual harm to come to yourself or others (born or unborn)?

__Yes. __No.

2. Is this fair?

__Yes. __No.

3. Is this honest?

__Yes. __No.

4. Is this legal?

__Yes. __No.

5. Could your choice invite more of God's blessings for your life?

__Yes. __No.

6. Could your decision cause financial loss for yourself or others?

__Yes. __No.

7. Will your choice please or grieve the Holy Spirit?

__Please. __Grieve.

8. Could your choice affect your freedom or the freedom of others?

__Yes. __No.

9. Will your choice bring lasting joy to God, others, and yourself?

__Yes. __No.

Comments:

_____

_____

_____

_____

_____

_____

_____

_____

_____

Next, we shall consider relationships, safety, conscience, finances, personal choices, and stereotypes.

* * *

---

[7] False Teachings By A Site Called "a True Church", http://www.catholic365.com/article/6411/false-teachings-by-a-site-called-a-true- (accessed September 01, 2018).

[8] False Teachings By A Site Called "a True Church", http://www.catholic365.com/article/6411/false-teachings-by-a-site-called-a-true- (accessed July 30, 2018).

"Your word *is* a lamp to my feet
And a light to my path" (Psalm 119:105 (NKJV)).

5
Long-Term Consequences

Choices are often about business, dating, health, education, debt, employment, finance, friendships, marriage, ministry, tithing, etcetera. God knows our associates' ways and opinions can influence us. That is why He put the following instructions in the Bible (Our Handbook for Life).

All or part of this passage may show up in other chapters because it is important to remember. (Belial is another name for Satan, which means *wicked and worthless*.)

> Do not be unequally yoked together with unbelievers. For what fellowship has righteousness with lawlessness?
>
> And what communion has light with darkness?
>
> —2 Corinthians 6:14 (NKJV)

> And what accord has Christ with Belial? Or what part has a believer with an unbeliever? And what agreement has the temple of God with idols? For you are the temple of the living God. As God has said:
>
> "I will dwell in them
> And walk among *them.*
> I will be their God,
> And they shall be My people."
>
> Therefore
>
> "Come out from among them
> And be separate, says the Lord.
> Do not touch what is unclean,
> And I will receive you."
>
> "I will be a Father to you,
> And you shall be My sons and daughters,
> Says the LORD Almighty."
>
> —2 Corinthians 6:15–18 (NKJV)

Relationships

Examine your relationship with Father God and with family, friends, and others.

1. How will the outcome of what you are considering affect your relationship with God?

It will be __helped. __hindered.

2. Will your action(s) honor God?

__Yes. __No. __Maybe.

3. How will your relationships with loved ones be affected?

They will be:

__happy. __disappointed.

— By Mary A. Bruno, Ph.D.

4. How will your relationships with other believers be impacted when they learn of your choice?

They will be:

__happy. __grieved.

5. How will your secular contacts be impacted?

__I will attract people to God.

__I will turn people away from God.

6. The secular world will want to:

__include me. __exclude me.

> And do not be conformed to this world, but be transformed by the renewing of your mind, that you may prove what *is* that good and acceptable and perfect will of God.
> —Romans 12:2 (NKJV)

> Even so let your light shine before men; that they may see your good works, and glorify your Father who is in heaven.   —Matthew 5:16 (ASV)

7. Consider your integrity. Will you be perceived as a better or more responsible person by doing this?

__Yes. __No.

> Or do you not know that your body is the temple of the Holy Spirit *who is* in you, whom you have from God, and you are not your own?
> For you were bought at a price; therefore glorify God in your body and in your spirit, which are God's.
> —1 Corinthians 6:19–20 (NKJV)

8. Your body belongs to God. Will doing this make you healthier?

__Yes. __No.

9. Do you want your children, nieces, nephews, or others to see and follow your example in this?

__Yes. __No.

10. If your action were to become the first link in a chain of godly or ungodly behavior, would your actions lead your loved ones and others closer to God, or away from God, and affect where they may spend eternity?

My example will lead them:

__closer to God. __away from God.

Pause and think about that.

> "But whoever causes one of these little ones who believe in Me to sin, it would be better for him if a millstone were hung around his neck, and he were drowned in the depth of the sea. Woe to the world because of offenses! For offenses must come, but woe to that man by whom the offense comes!"
> —Matthew 18:6–7 (NKJV)

> Whoever therefore breaks one of the least of these commandments, and teaches men so, shall be called least in the kingdom of heaven; but whoever does and teaches *them*, he shall be called great in the kingdom of heaven.   —Matthew 5:19 (NKJV)

Safety

> Be sober, be watchful: your adversary the devil, as a roaring lion, walketh about, seeking whom he may devour:
> —1 Peter 5:8 (ASV)

1. Could this choice lead to a habit that would weaken your health, muddle your thinking, lower your quality of life, or lead to death?

__Yes. __No. __ Probably.

2. Could this decision become a habit that that will renew your strength and increase God's blessings for the rest of your life and the lives of others?

__Yes. __No. __ Probably.

3. Could this choice become a habit that would devour your health, strength, time, and finances, and weaken your efficiency?

__Yes. __No. __Probably.

Time

1. Will this choice provide more time for your career and/or to serve God?

__Yes. __No. __Maybe.

2. Will this decision free-up more quality time to be with loved ones?

__Yes. __No. __Maybe.

3. Will doing this make you more productive?

__Yes. __No. __Maybe.

Note: When considering a choice for your education substitute, "education" or "study" for "work" for each of the following questions.

4. Will you have more or fewer work hours?

__Yes. __No. __Maybe.

Please write how many:

_____More work hours

_____per month

_____per year

_____Fewer work hours

_____ per month, _

_____per year

5. Stop and think! Will this change affect your travel hours and expense to and from work?

__Yes. __No. __Maybe.

Please calculate the differences in travel hours and the financial impact of traveling to and from work:

_____more travel hours for work per month

_____more travel hours for work per year

_____fewer travel hours for work per month

_____fewer travel hours for work per year

$_____increased travel expense per month

$_____increased travel expense per year

$_____ decreased travel costs per month

$_____ decreased travel expense per year

Conscience

God has made our conscience sensitive to what is right and wrong. As we walk closely with the LORD, His inner voice will incline our hearts to walk uprightly as we obey His Word and follow the Holy Spirit's leading.

1. How will your conscience like what you are considering?

__Let's shout it to the world!

__Don't tell anyone!

__I will use a habit (TV, music, alcohol, drugs, games, overeating, etc.) to dull my conscience until I can no longer hear or recognize God's voice and leading.

Finances

Will going forward with this opportunity strengthen your financial ability to advance your education, career, or other goals?

__ Yes. __No. __Maybe.

Getting one's finances in order begins with God's tithe. To *tithe* is to give God ten percent of one's income (increase), which is ten cents from every dollar. Then, if not already doing so, a person could save at least ten percent for retirement and ten percent to save or invest and live on the rest. God's Word is very clear about tithing because that is what He wants us to do (to pay) every week.

> "Will a man rob God?
> Yet you have robbed Me!
> "But you say,
> 'In what way have we robbed You?'
> In tithes and offerings.
> You are cursed with a curse,
> For you have robbed Me,
> *Even* this whole nation.
> Bring all the tithes into
> the storehouse,"
> That there may be food in My house,
> And try Me now in this,"
> Says the LORD of hosts,
>
> "If I will not open for you
> the windows of heaven
> And pour out for you *such* blessing
> That *there will* not *be room* enough
> *to receive it."*
> —Malachi 3:8–10 (NKJV)

Curses

Some have heard reports of people being under curses. Malachi 3:9 shows that robbing God of His tithes and offerings brought a curse upon the tithe-stealers. A wise one may want to pay his or her full ten percent, have God's long-term blessings, and avoid the curse.

Non-tithers may not know that giving to God brings tremendous joy. Tithing is easy to do; just set the funds aside until it is time to attend a worship service. This means you will show up to your place of

Choices & Strongholds

— By Mary A. Bruno, Ph.D.

worship and put your entire tithe in the offering plate. If you are physically unable to go to a church, it is better to mail or send your tithe than not to pay it.

If you are not already a tither, are you ready to start now?

__Yes. __No. __Maybe.

> "And I will rebuke the devourer for your sakes,
> So that he will not destroy the fruit of your ground,
> Nor shall the vine fail to bear fruit for you in the field,"
> Says the LORD of hosts;
> "And all nations will call you blessed,
> For you will be a delightful land,"
> Says the LORD of hosts.
> —Malachi 3:11–12 (NKJV)

You may try or think you can get away with it, but you will never ever be able to out-give God. Never!

I have tried to do so for years, and He keeps on giving back in surprising ways. Recently one of my daughters and I obeyed God's nudge to drive up to Morro Bay, California, to pray, blow the shofar by the Morro Rock, hand out gospel tracts and talk to people about Jesus. It was a 302-mile drive (about 6 hours) each way. On the way home, we got on a toll road, did not see where to pay a fee, and kept driving.

A bill came in the mail for the $6.22 toll fee. Another envelope in that batch of mail had a refund check from a medical facility for $6.52. God not only picked up the tab for our $6.22 toll but gave us an extra 30 cents to invest back into His kingdom. We knew that He was having fun while assuring us that because the trip was His idea, He covered the toll fee. Bless Him!

Tattoos and Piercings

Most people's preferences change over time. The tricycle that was great when you were young may seem laughable when ready for a flashy sports car. One's trendy tattoos, especially gang tattoos, or the name of a former sweetheart, may be unwanted after time. Undergoing tattoo removal is painful and costly.

Body piercing, once "in vogue," may look out of place in a business setting. It is wise to do nothing to your body that cannot be undone, or will leave a mark or scar.

Bear in mind that your virginity can only be given once. Your husband or wife will appreciate it if your once-in-a-life-time gift is reserved for your honeymoon.

Have no fear if the deeds have been done. It will take more than an ink gun or piercing tool to stop God's love and anointing from flowing through His dedicated servants. I know a missionary, covered with big colorful "ink." He walks in God's love, wins souls, evicts dem-

Choices & Strongholds

— By Mary A. Bruno, Ph.D.

ons, trains leaders, and rejoices when God heals the sick.

Labels/ Stereotypes

Sometimes, due to the things we say or do, others may consider us to be (label us) part of a particular group or crowd. This can be a good thing or a bad thing, depending on our associates. Therefore, we must choose our friends wisely.

1. Do you think this choice will cause you to be identified with those whose lives please God?

__Yes. __No. __Maybe.

2. If you proceed with this, what kind of group may claim you as "One of us?"

__ Godly	__ Ungodly
__ Addicts	__ Alcoholics
__ Ministers	__ Athletes
__ Criminals	__ Professionals
__ Unwed parents	__Gangs

3. Could what you are considering make you more or less valuable in the job market?

__More valuable. __Less valuable.

4. Will your choice be worth the price(s) that you must pay?

__Yes. __No. __Maybe.

5. If it looks like a wolf, walks like a wolf, howls like a wolf, and bites like a wolf, it is probably a wolf (possibly in sheep's clothing). Does this person or opportunity resemble a wolf?

__Yes. __No. __Maybe.

6.__True. __False.

It has sharp teeth, a bushy tail, chases creatures, and howls often, but I'm still not convinced.

7. Do you think God wants you in this group?

__Yes. __No. __Maybe.

Doors

1. Will desirable long-term opportunities open or close to you as a result of your decision?

__Open. __Close.

2. Will your choice please, and bring glory to God?

__Yes. __No. __Maybe.

3. Jot down how some of the long-range effects of your decision (with which you must live) will impact your future and that of others in:

five years. _____

_____

ten years. _____

_____

twenty years. _____

_____

_____

Next: dating and marriage.
***

"Your word *is* a lamp to my feet
And a light to my path" (Psalm 119:105 (NKJV)).

6
Dating and Marriage —Part 1

While learning to think things through, we must address dating. Most of us want our romantic choices to bring lasting love, joy, and peace. Is the fact that a person is cute or handsome, reason enough to make a permanent vow? It has been said, "Beauty fades, but dumb is forever." Those who will bypass superficial relationships and wait for God's lasting blessings in a delightful faith-based romantic commitment may appreciate this chapter.

The following questions will help you to test a relationship to find your level of compatibility and expectation of God's blessing regarding the person you are dating, which usually implies a candidate for marriage. (Avoid dating anyone you should not marry!) These questions may also apply to business or ministry commitments.

> Behold, how good and how pleasant it is
> For brethren to dwell together in unity!
> —Psalm 133:1 (ASV)

1. Are you both born-again believers in Jesus Christ?

__Yes. __No.

2. Do you read the Bible and pray together regularly?

__Yes. __No.

> Do not be unequally yoked together with unbelievers. For what fellowship has righteousness with lawlessness? And what communion has light with darkness?
> —2 Corinthians 6:14 (NKJV)

> And if a house be divided against itself, that house will not be able to stand. —Mark 3:25 (ASV)

Unequal Yokes

God tells believers not to be unequally yoked together with unbelievers. This is a *command* — *Not a suggestion!*—given to steer God's children away from years of misery, conflict, lost ministry opportunities, and from possibly losing their souls.

1. Does he (or she) display heartfelt love for the Lord Jesus Christ?

__Yes. __No.

2. Do you have similar or complimentary spiritual desires and callings?

__Yes. __No.

3. Are you similar in mental and spiritual maturity?

__Yes. __No.

> Shall two walk together, except they have agreed?   —Amos 3:3 (ASV)

> But He, knowing their thoughts, said to them: "Every kingdom divided against itself is brought to desolation, and a house *divided* against a house falls."   —Luke 11:17 (NKJV)

4. Do you both attend a house of worship weekly and pay God's tithe?

__Yes. __No.

5. Does your relationship have guilt-free peace and holy joy?

__Yes. __No.

6. Do you embrace harmonious life goals and similar social status?

__Yes. __No.

7. Do you both show respect for one another other by staying well-groomed?

__Yes. __No.

8. Are you physically attracted to him or her?

__Yes. __No.

9. Do you love his or her vehicle, possessions, position, and wealth more than you love him or her?

__Yes. __No.

10. Are you both able to earn a comfortable living without receiving financial help from your parents?

__Yes. __No.

> Therefore a man shall leave his father and mother and be joined to his wife, and they shall become one flesh.   —Genesis 2:24 (ASV)

For New Testament references on this subject, see: Matthew 19:5, Mark 10:7, and Ephesians 5:31.

God's plan for married couples is to leave their parents' house, pay their own way, and establish a separate family unit.

11. We both enjoy similar kinds of

__food __sports __music.

12. Do you both agree regarding establishing a family and spiritual training for your children?

__Yes. __No.

> Do you have faith? Have *it* to yourself before God. Happy *is* he who does not condemn himself in what he approves.
> —Romans 14:22 (NKJV)

13. Do you want your sons or daughters to resemble him or her in looks, character, and habits?

— By Mary A. Bruno, Ph.D.

__Yes. __No.

14. Are you similar enough to not be perceived as "the odd couple"?

__Yes. __No.

> A good man out of the good treasure of his heart brings forth good; and an evil man out of the evil treasure of his heart brings forth evil. For out of the abundance of the heart his mouth speaks.
> —Luke 6:45 (NKJV)

15. What kind of attitude does he or she exhibit?

___ Positive and uplifting.

___ Negative and grouchy.

16. Would you like to be around that kind of attitude forever?

__Yes. __No.

17. Does he or she usually encourage or criticize you or others?

__Encourage. __Criticize.

18. Would you like to be around his or her kind of talk (encouragement or criticism) forever?

__Yes. __No.

19. Does this person use profane or vulgar language?

__Yes. __No.

If he or she does, is that acceptable to you?

__Yes. __No.

20. After having done wrong, is this person swift to own up to it, apolo-gize, ask forgiveness, and make lasting and long-term changes?

__Yes. __No.

21. Would you like to be around more of that kind of character and attitude for all of your days?

__Yes. __No.

22. Does he or she show respect by listening patiently without interrupting when you express your thoughts or feelings?

__Yes. __No.

Look Deeper

In the verses below, please circle the spiritual fruit that is evident in his or her life.

> But the fruit of the Spirit is love, joy, peace, longsuffering, kindness, goodness, faithfulness, meekness, self-control; against such there is no law.   —Galatians 5:22–23 (ASV)

1. Is this person kind or mean to animals?

He or she is ___kind. ___mean.

2. Is he or she polite to you and others at home and in public?

__Yes. __No.

3. Are you delighted to be seen with him or her when he or she exhibits that kind of behavior?

__Yes. __No.

As godly character surfaces in the daily life of one who walks closely with Jesus, the fruit of the Spirit makes life much sweeter for all around him or her.

4. Does the person you are dating embarrass you by scolding sales-people and demanding they bring whatever he/she wants?

__Yes. __No.

5. Would you like to be around that kind of conduct for many more years to come?

__Yes. __No.

Warning!

Actions rarely change. This is why it is wise to know a person for at least a year *before* making a long-term commitment.

After about three months into a relationship, behavior patterns may show up that cause concern but get overlooked. After six months, more bad habits or undesirable mindsets surface, for which excuses may be made. After nine months, new causes for concern appear during times of anger or when things are not going his or her way. And if you, my friend, are still around after a year, the other person will probably reveal different hidden opinions, habits, tendencies, or preferences that may worsen over time.

On the other hand, during these waiting periods, the relationship may become like mining for gold, with delightful new characteristics coming to light with each new day.

A wise one will never regret having waited a year to trust but prove a relationship. If it works out—Great! They can walk down the aisle together, and if not, each will still be free to walk away.

> *As* a ring of gold in a swine's snout, *So is* a fair woman that is without discretion. —Proverbs 11:22 (ASV)

1. Is he or she addicted to tobacco, alcohol, pornography, gambling, drugs, sex, or gaming, etc., or has he or she been unfaithful to you?

__Yes. __No.

If the answer was "Yes," does he or she want to keep wallowing in the sin or addiction, or does he or she want to ask and receive God's help to get free and stay free?

__ He or she wants to wallow in sin.

__ He or she wants God's help to get clean and stay clean.

2. Are you willing to invest your time, emotions, savings, and income to support his or her habits, and all of the health, legal, and financial problems that come with them for the rest of your life?

__Yes. __No.

> Who can find a virtuous wife?
> For her worth *is* far above rubies.
> The heart of her husband safely trusts her; So he will have no lack of gain.
> She does him good and not evil
> All the days of her life.
> —Proverbs 31:10–12 (NKJV)

— By Mary A. Bruno, Ph.D.

other has finished a different shift and needs to sleep or rest?[9]

__Yes. __No.

4. Does he or she make time to be with you?

__Yes. __No.

5. Are you happy to be seen with him/ her in public?

__Yes. __No.

Alcohol

> Do not mix with winebibbers,
> *Or* with gluttonous eaters of meat;
> —Proverbs 23:20 (NKJV)

> Do not look on the wine when it is red,
> When it sparkles in the cup,
> *When* it swirls around smoothly;
> At the last it bites like a serpent,
> And stings like a viper.
> —Proverbs 23:31–32 (NKJV)

Do you and he or she agree with Father God about not drinking alcoholic beverages?

__Yes. __No.

If you answered "No," please consider how Father God probably feels about your ongoing involvement with someone who defies His Holy Word, and if you will choose to please God or the other person.

> And even these reel with wine, and stagger with strong drink; the priest and the prophet reel with strong drink, they are swallowed up of wine, they stagger with strong drink; they err in vision, they stumble in judgment.   — Isaiah 28:7 (ASV)

> And be not drunken with wine, wherein is riot, but be filled with the Spirit; speaking one to another in psalms and hymns and spiritual songs, singing and making melody with your heart to the Lord;
> —Ephesians 5:18–19 (ASV)

Tip!

A little sip of the "Bubble-EEE" can lead to big "Trouble-EEE."

Comments:

_____

_____

_____

_____

_____

To be continued.

* * *

---

[9] Seizing The Future - Achieve,
   https://www.achieve.org/files/Achieve_OHcareerTech.pdf (accessed July 29, 2018).

"Your word *is* a lamp to my feet
And a light to my path" (Psalm 119:105 (NKJV)).

7

Dating and Marriage —Part 2

We shall continue to examine and test relationships to learn if there is a healthy level of compatibility and expectation of God's blessing regarding a lasting commitment to the one you are dating (marriage candidate). As mentioned previously, these questions may also apply to business or ministry commitments.

> For there is nothing hid, save that it should be manifested; neither was *anything* made secret, but that it should come to light.
> —Mark 4:22 (ASV)

Things were, literally, not adding up right when Rocco and I were running a secular business. We could not figure out why, and prayed, "LORD, please show us what we need to see and know." —And did He ever!

Evidence started showing up all over the place, such as a note by the cash register where a cashier had been recording his thefts, and empty currency containers where another cashier had been robbing our safe. More printed evidence with video records revealed additional illegal activities that had created an enormous loss. We made major changes that resolved the problem.

So, as you can see, my friend, it is essential to ask Jesus to show what you need to know regarding personal, business, and ministry relationships, and what you need to do about that information. We still pray that kind of prayer often.

The LORD is faithful to reveal facts that need to be known and understood. Sometimes this brings joy, and sometimes it prevents grief.

1. Have you asked God to reveal everything you need to know about the person in your life?

__Yes. __No.
  If so, what did you discover?

___ Admirable qualities.

___ Causes for concern.

2. Have you asked Father God to show you whether or not you have His blessing to marry or make a commitment to this person?

__Yes. __No.

— By Mary A. Bruno, Ph.D.

> "You shall have no other gods before Me. " —Exodus 20:3 (NKJV)

3. Has he or she asked you to please him or her, by committing a crime, or sin, or doing what God forbids?

__Yes. __No.

If your answer was "Yes," whom did you choose to please?

__ Him. __ Her. ___ God.

4. Has he or she ever put your safety at risk by driving unsafely while angry or under the influence of alcohol or drugs, or shaken a fist, wielded a weapon, or made threats?

__Yes. __No.

5. Has he or she said or done anything that[10] (saddened) your heart and grieved the Holy Spirit?

__Yes. __No.

Do you want to endure more of that kind of talk and conduct for the rest of your life?

__Yes. __No.

6. Jesus, Prince of Peace, leads in paths of peace, love, joy, and righteousness. Do you have peace about continuing this relationship?

__Yes. __No.

Face the Facts (Again)

In the passage below, circle all works of the flesh (again) that are evident in his or her life.

> The cravings of the self-life are obvious: Sexual immorality, lustful thoughts, pornography, chasing after things instead of God, manipulating others, hatred of those who get in your way, senseless arguments, resentment when others are favored, temper tantrums, angry quarrels, only thinking of yourself, being in love with your own opinions, being envious of the blessings of others, murder, uncontrolled addictions, wild parties, and all other similar behavior.
>
> Haven't I already warned you that those who use their "freedom" for these things will not inherit the kingdom realm of God!
> —Galatians 5:19–21
> The Passion Translation (TPT)

The LORD makes it clear that those who do those things will not be in His kingdom. That only leaves one other place for them to spend eternity. Be careful that you do not end up there with him/her/them!

> And if any was not found written in the book of life, he was cast into the lake of fire. —Revelation 20:15 (ASV)

1. Does he or she exhibit Christ-like behavior? (Can you imagine Jesus saying or doing what he, she, or they said or did?)

__Yes. __No.

2. Do you respect or often find fault with him or her?

__ Respect. __ Find fault.

Violence

Listen up! If we like people, we do not curse, hit, or hurt them or their loved ones, pets, or possessions. If someone has threatened or slapped, pushed, punched, struck, choked, kicked, pulled your hair, or hurt you or a loved one—he or she was not sent by God! *Get away and stay away*—before you become disfigured or killed! Threats or violent behavior are not from God.

The behavior of an abuser who does not surrender himself or herself to Jesus Christ and make Him Lord of his or her life usually worsens over time.

Many victims have stayed with their violence-prone "mates" while hoping and praying the abuse would stop.—Which it did—when their murdered bodies lay cold, stiff, and voiceless in the grave, while the abuser moved on to his or her next prey.

If you are in a violent relationship and want out, Jesus will make a way to escape and will help you to recover and find peace within God's family. He will give you pastors after His own heart, who will feed you with knowledge and understanding. He will help you to grow in grace with sweet peace, safety, and joy.

> And the King will answer and say to them, 'Assuredly, I say to you, inasmuch as you did *it* to one of the least of these My brethren, you did *it* to Me.' —Matthew 25:40 (NKJV)

> Husbands, love your wives, even as Christ also loved the church, and gave himself up for it;
> —Ephesians 5:25 (ASV)

1. Has he or she ever harmed you, or your loved one or pet, or damaged your or their personal property?

__Yes. __No.

> Make no friendship with an angry man,
> And with a furious man do not go,
> —Proverbs 22:24 (NKJV)

> An angry man stirs up strife,
> And a furious man abounds in transgression. —Proverbs 29:22 (NKJV)

2. Has he or she ever hit you, shook you, left bruises or red marks on your body, given you a black eye, caused you to bleed, shouted profanities at you, thrown things at you, hit walls, brandished a weapon in your presence, or threatened to harm or kill you?

__Yes. __No.

If so, do you really want to endure this kind of behavior for the rest of your life?

Choices & Strongholds

— By Mary A. Bruno, Ph.D.

__Yes. __No.

> There is no fear in love; but perfect love casts out fear, because fear involves torment. But he who fears has not been made perfect in love.
> —1 John 4:18 (NKJV)

3. Are you afraid of him or her?

__Yes. __No.

4. Do you trust his or her ability to make wise and godly decisions to protect and keep you safe and at peace?

__Yes. __No.

5. Do you think he or she will stand by you and seek God's help in times of trouble?

__Yes. __No.

6. If he or she has a criminal record, do you think it may prevent you from reaching your goals?

__Yes. __No. ____Maybe.

Note: The person God wants to share your life in marriage will protect you, build you up, and help you to serve God. He or she will ask you to do nothing that would displease God, violate His Word, break laws of the land, or put your health at risk. The one with God's approval will not humiliate or harm you or your relatives, pets, or possessions. He or she will not scream or swear at you, threaten, shake, violate, or belittle you, call

you nasty names, or ridicule your faith in God.

The one God has for you will build your relationship according to God's Word, in peace, love, joy, and holiness as he or she lovingly takes your hand and urges, "Oh, magnify the LORD with me, and let us exalt His name together" (Psalm 34:3).

> Husbands, love your wives, just as Christ also loved the church and gave Himself for her, that He might sanctify and cleanse her with the washing of water by the word, that He might present her to Himself a glorious church, not having spot or wrinkle or any such thing, but that she should be holy and without blemish. So husbands ought to love their own wives as their own bodies; he who loves his wife loves himself. For no one ever hated his own flesh, but nourishes and cherishes it, just as the Lord *does* the church. For we are members of His body, of His flesh and of His bones. "For this reason a man shall leave his father and mother and be joined to his wife, and the two shall become one flesh." This is a great mystery, but I speak concerning Christ and the church. Nevertheless let each one of you in particular so love his own wife as himself, and let the wife *see* that she respects *her* husband.
> —Ephesians 5:25–33 (NKJV)

If the one whom you are dating or considering for marriage does not meet God's standards, he or she is a counterfeit and is not the right one for you.

Other Considerations

> 'Honor your father and your mother, as the LORD your God has commanded you, that your days may be long, and that it may be well with you in the land which the LORD your God is giving you.'
> —Deuteronomy 5:16a (NKJV)

1. ___True. ___False.

He or she demonstrates love and respect for his or her parents or guardians, which, according to Deuteronomy 5:16 (shown above), is God's key to a good life, a long life, and for owning land.

2. ___True. ___False.

I asked my godly parents or guardians and my pastor for their advice about dating him or her.

3. ___True. ___False.

We will receive biblical marriage counseling.

4. ___True. ___False.

I believe God is very pleased with our relationship and will bless us.

5. ___True. ___False.

I will put my will first and follow what God forbids. I will suffer years of bitter and constant regrets, with grief for loved ones and me— because I choose to defy God's laws and walk in the flesh. I will have no peace, and my life will become a living *hell on earth.*

6. ___True. ___False.

I will put a stop to this unwise relationship now, wait for God's timing, and make room in my life for the one whom God will bring to me at His appointed time and place.

7. ___True. ___False.

Because I will choose that which Father God approves and will refuse all that He warns against and will not bless, my life will overflow with His kindness, mercy, and glorious blessings.

> Show me Your ways, O LORD;
> Teach me Your paths.
> Lead me in Your truth and teach me,
> For You *are* the God of my salvation;
> On You I wait all the day.
> —Psalm 25:4–5 (NKJV)

> I waited patiently for the LORD;
> And He inclined to me,
> And heard my cry.
> He also brought me up out of a
> Horrible pit—, Out of the miry clay,
> And set my feet upon a rock,
> *And* established my steps.
> He has put a new song in my mouth—
> Praise to our God;
> Many will see *it* and fear,
> And will trust in the LORD.
> —Psalm 40:1–3 (NKJV)

> "Therefore whoever hears these sayings of Mine, and does them, I will liken him to a wise man who built his house on the rock: and the rain descended, the floods came, and the winds blew and beat on that house; and it did not fall, for it was founded on the rock.
>
> "But everyone who hears these sayings of Mine, and does not do them, will be like a foolish man who built his house on the sand: and the rain descended, the floods came, and the winds blew and beat on that house; and it fell. And great was its fall."
>
> —Matthew 7:24–27 (NKJV)

8. __True. __False.

Like the wise man who builds his house on the rock, I choose to follow God's lead and enjoy His sweet love, peace, joy, health, and prosperity.

Comments:

_____

_____

_____

_____

_____

_____

_____

_____

_____

_____

_____

_____

_____

Next, Father God will help you to make excellent choices.

* * *

---

[10] How To Play "let's Pretend" Like A Pro With Your Child .., http://www.chaoticlifeoflauren.com/pretend-play/ (accessed July 30, 2018).

"Your word *is* a lamp to my feet
And a light to my path" (Psalm 119:105 (NKJV)).

8
God Will Help You to Choose

The verses in Proverbs 3:1–18 abound with Father God's supreme wisdom for His kingdom children. Expect Him to reveal sweet new understanding with the study of each passage.

Please, highlight or circle the most meaningful words and phrases while answering questions for the Bible verses in this chapter.

> My son, do not forget my law,
> But let your heart keep my commands;
> For length of days and long life
> And peace they will add to you.
> —Proverbs 3:1–2 (NKJV)

Wise Up

1. God's three rewards for remembering His Law and keeping His commandments in our hearts are[11] length of _____, long _____and _____.

2. Please, highlight or circle the words and phrases that are most meaningful to[12] you in the following passage.

> Let not mercy and truth forsake you;
> Bind them around your neck,
> Write them on the tablet of your heart,
> *And* so find favor and high esteem
> In the sight of God and man.
> —Proverbs 3:3–4 (NKJV)

God's two rewards for embracing and adorning ourselves with His mercy and truth and writing them on our hearts are: We will find _____ and high _____ in the sight of _____ and _____.

3. Highlight or circle the words and phrases that are most meaningful to you in the following passage.

> Trust in the LORD with all your heart,
> And lean not on your own understanding;
> In all your ways acknowledge Him,
> And He shall direct your paths.
> —Proverbs 3:5–6 (NKJV)

4. God's reward for trusting in Him with all of our heart and acknow-

ledging Him in all of our ways is: He will _____ our paths. But, it is our responsibility to follow (to or from) where ever God leads.

5. Please highlight or circle the words and phrases that are most meaningful to you in this passage.

> Do not be wise in your own eyes;
> Fear the LORD and depart from evil.
> It will be health to your flesh,
> And strength to your bones.
> —Proverbs 3:7—8 (NKJV)

6. The reward for not being wise in our own eyes, but fearing (honoring) God and departing from evil is: _____ to our _____ and _____ to our _____.

7. Please highlight [13]or circle words and phrases that are most meaningful to you in the following passages.[14]

> Honor the LORD with your possessions,
> And with the firstfruits of all your increase;
> So your barns will be filled with plenty,
> And your vats will overflow with new wine. —Proverbs 3:9–10 (NKJV)

8. God's Word tells us to honor Him with our possessions, and first-fruits of *all* of our increase (pay-

checks, etc.) so that our barns[15] (where we keep our valuables) will be _____ with _____ and our _____ will overflow with new _____ (a type of new joy).

> Upon the first day of the week let each one of you lay by him in store, as he may prosper, that no collections be made when I come.
> —1 Corinthians 16:2 (ASV)

9. According to 1 Corinthians 16:2, which day of the week is designated for laying aside (to put down, carry no longer, lay aside money[16]) our offerings?

__ First day. __Third day.

__Seventh day.

10. Highlight or circle the words and phrases that are most meaningful to you in this passage.

> My son, do not despise the chastening of the LORD,
> Nor detest His correction;
> For whom the LORD loves He corrects,
> Just as a father the son *in whom* he delights. —Proverbs 3:11–12 (NKJV)

11. Being chastened (corrected and taught of the Lord) assures believers that we are God's

_____ and He _____ in us.

Please tell about when Father God corrected you; how you felt about it then and how you feel about it now.

_____

_____

_____

12. Please highlight or circle all of the words and phrases that are the most meaningful to you in the following passage.

> Happy *is* the man *who* finds wisdom,
> And the man *who* gains understanding;
>
> For her proceeds *are* better than the profits of silver,
> And her gain than fine gold.
>
> She *is* more precious than rubies,
> And all the things you may desire cannot compare with her.
>
> Length of days *is* in her right hand,
> In her left hand riches and honor.
> Her ways *are* ways of pleasantness,
> And all her paths *are* peace.
> She *is* a tree of life to those who take hold of her,
> And happy *are all* who retain her.
> —Proverbs 3:13–18 (NKJV)

Wisdom and Understanding's Rewards

Nine of wisdom and understanding's rewards are:

1. Her proceeds are better than the profits of _____.

2. Her gain is better than fine _____.

3. She is more precious than _____.

4. All the things you may

_____ cannot be

_____ with her.

5. _____ of _____ is in her right hand.

6. In her _____ are riches and honor.

7. Her ways are _____ of _____.

8. She is a _____ of _____ to those who take hold of her.

9. All her paths are _____. _____ are _____ who retain her.

The Prince of Peace leads His own in paths of peace.

10. Do you have peace about the path you are considering?

__Yes. __No.

Review Your Motives

Check your heart for pride, greed, rebellion, or vindictiveness (wish to get even). It is time to pray, inspect your motivations, dump any sin, habits, or ungodly ways that Father

God brings to mind, and make room for the new and better things that He wants to bring into your life.

St. John tells how to get clean again. Please highlight or draw a circle around the most important words and phrases in this verse:

> If we confess our sins, he is faithful and righteous to forgive us our sins, and to cleanse us from all unrighteousness.   —1 John 1:9 (ASV)

If you notice anything in your life that you need to mention to God, always remember He has been waiting for you to tell Him about it, receive His cleansing forgiveness, and trade your weakness for His strength. This is a great time to forgive all who have wronged you, and (of course) pay your tithes.

Somehow it seems more logical to expect the LORD to hear and answer our prayers when we are honest, merciful, and current with our giving. He rewards our obedience. Interestingly, practicing self-control when it comes to paying our tithes overflows into practicing self-control in many other areas, which keeps us walking victoriously through temptations and tests.

There is hope! This is no time to wallow in guilt and condemnation over dumb mistakes. If you did wrong, own up to it; confess it to Father God; break up with it, accept

God's restoration, make a serious effort to do better next time, and then, get on with your life. Jesus can keep you from falling. (Jude, 24). What more could we ask?

> Now unto him that is able to guard you from stumbling, and to set you before the presence of his glory without blemish in exceeding joy, to the only God our Saviour, through Jesus Christ our Lord, *be* glory, majesty, dominion and power, before all time, and now, and for evermore. Amen.   —Jude 24–25 (ASV)

Start Now

It is time, my friend, to rise up, own up, clean up, cheer up, hurry up, and keep up your walk with the Lord! Then, boldly dare to help restore, and encourage others, who may have fallen back or strayed into enemy territory, while being careful to avoid the enemy's snares.

After heartfelt prayer and reviewing the facts, a child of God will be better able to recognize God's will. (If the LORD has given you a prayer language, this would be an ideal time to use it.) In the following passage, the Apostle Paul mentioned singing and praying with the spirit and with the understanding.

Please highlight or circle the most meaningful words in the following verses.

> For if I pray in a tongue, my spirit prays, but my understanding is unfruitful.
> What is *the conclusion* then? I will pray with the spirit, and I will also pray with the understanding. I will sing with the spirit, and I will also sing with the understanding.
> —1 Corinthians 14:14–15 (NKJV)

When you finally have God's peace, love, and joy flowing through your spirit regarding the matter that you are considering, that would be an ideal time to pray and make your decision. Then, put it in writing and trust Father God to help you to follow through. He understands what kind of a step this is for you, and will be there to steady you and remind you of His promises when doubts arise or challenges come.

Choose

I have carefully considered God's leading and guidance from His Word, and other information regarding the following opportunity:

_____

_____

_____

I have decided to:

_____

_____

_____

_____

_____

I will do this before

____:____ ____a.m. ____p.m. on

Date_____.

Follow-up

To reinforce my commitments and see them through, I will do the following by ____:____ ____a.m. ____p.m. on (date) _____.

_____

_____

_____

Get ready to set godly goals.

***

[11] Authenticity: Why Being Unvarnished Matters | Project Eve, https://projecteve.com/why-being-unvarnished-matters/ (accessed July 29, 2018).

[12] Proverbs 3:1 - My Son, Do Not Forget My Teaching, But Keep .., https://www.biblestudytools.com/proverbs/3-1-compare.html (accessed July 29, 2018).

[13] Authenticity: Why Being Unvarnished Matters | Project Eve, https://projecteve.com/why-being-unvarnished-matters/ (accessed July 31, 2018)

[14] Romans 12:16 Live In Harmony With One Another. Do Not Be .., http://biblehub.com/romans/12-16.htm (accessed July 30, 2018).

[15] Art Bead Scene Blog: Inspired By Music, http://artbeadscene.blogspot.com/2013/02/inspired-by-music.html (accessed September 01, 2018).

[16] "G5087 - tithēmi - Strong's Greek Lexicon (KJV)." Blue Letter Bible. Accessed 25 Nov, 2018. https://www.blueletterbible.org//lang/Lexicon/Lexicon.cfm?Strongs=G5087&t=KJV

"Your word *is* a lamp to my feet
And a light to my path" (Psalm 119:105 (NKJV)).

9
Set New Goals

Let's establish and document some realistic, measurable, and attainable goals. Practical planning is vital. It has been said, "If you aim at nothing, you will be sure to hit it."

The Scriptures remind us that, "Where there is no vision the people perish . . ." (Proverbs 29:18 KJV). The secret to successful goal-setting is to discover what God will or will not bless; then consider the options; dump the bad; keep the good; and plan accordingly. Joyous blessings await the discerning person who can identify when an opportunity is or is not from the LORD, and choose that which has His approval.

"Vision" in Proverbs 29:18, has to do with divine communication, such as when the Holy Spirit illuminates a passage of Scripture to one's heart, or an anointed person brings a message from God.

> Where there is no vision [no revelation of God and His word], the people are unrestrained;
> But happy *and* blessed is he who keeps the law [of God].
> —Proverbs 29:18
> Amplified Bible (AMP)

When Father God leads anyone to do something, it will be in harmony with His written Word. He will bless the individual and whatever He leads him or her to do, and will manifest His Presence, power, and provision with peace in the matter.

Father God has committed Himself to His people, and calls for His people to separate themselves from unbelievers and idols.

As mentioned earlier, Belial, another name for Satan, means *wicked and worthless.*

> And what concord hath Christ with Belial? or what portion hath a believer with an unbeliever? And what agreement hath a temple of God with idols? for we are a temple of the living God; even as God said, I will dwell in them, and walk in them; and I will be their God, and they shall be my people. Wherefore
> Come ye out from among them, and be ye separate, saith the Lord,
> And touch no unclean thing;
> And I will receive you,
> —2 Corinthians 6:15–17 (ASV)

> And will be to you a Father,
> And ye shall be to me sons and daughters,
> saith the Lord Almighty.
> —2 Corinthians 6:18 (ASV)

When Father God says to not do something ("touch not" etc.), He will not lead anyone to do it, and will not bless it —no matter how deeply in love you are, or how good it may look, sound, taste, feel, or seem to one's carnal and self-serving mind.

When Father God says, "Do not touch" something, He means, "Keep your hands off! Leave it alone! Get away from it! Turn away and stay from the nasty thing—before it destroys you!"

If you want to look old and wrinkled in a hurry, just dive into sin or addictions and watch the wrinkles rush in like ants at a picnic to devour your good looks.

The LORD'S commands to "touch not" are not negotiable! A wise person who values His blessing will obey God and stay away from that which is forbidden. He or she will not admire, caress, participate in, or linger by that which Father God condemns, but instead, will cling to all that is pure and holy, will honor and obey the LORD, and will walk away with a clean heart. He or she will enjoy God's lingering peace and rewards on earth and thru eternity.

Realistic and Measurable Goals

These examples of realistic, measurable, specific, and attainable goals may be helpful when writing your goals, which, of course, will be different.

1. Accept honest employment within 30 days.

2. Teach the dog a new trick this month.

3. Clean out the garage before January.

4. Lose 10 pounds before June.

5. Email, text, or call Mom and Dad or _____ weekly.

6. Learn to use a computer by June 30.

7. Prayerfully share God's plan of salvation with twelve (or more) people this year.

> Delight yourself also in the LORD,
> And He shall give you the desires of your heart.   —Psalm 37:4 (NKJV)

Before writing your goals, please consult the LORD, review the sample pages, and then complete the goals form in the Appendix. Your goals should be realistic, achievable, measurable, and attainable that you can accomplish within the designated year.

✓ It is wise to begin by reminding Jesus that He is appreciated and welcome in your life.

Choices & Strongholds

— By Mary A. Bruno, Ph.D.

✓ Then dig deep down into your heart of hearts. Talk to Father God about any plans you have considered while reading the previous chapters. (He already knows your thoughts and desires, but will like hearing about them from you.)

✓ Next, review God's tips, commands, cautions, and promises in the following Scriptures, and comment on how to apply them.

While teaching His disciples about Father God's joyous generosity to them, Jesus said:

> For where your treasure is, there your heart will be also.
> —Luke 12:34 (NKJV)

Note: Jesus, Father God's Greatest Treasure, with His Gifts and the Fruit of His Spirit, are in us—His children. And where Father God's treasure is, there will His heart be also (with us). How precious!

As good stewards of God's blessings, we get to set goals, not only for earthly rewards, but to invest our time, talents, and assets into God's Kingdom. For instance, in 1 Kings 2:1-3, David's advice to his son Solomon, and Solomon's obedience to God's Word made Solomon wiser and more prosperous than any other king.

> Now the days of David drew near that he should die, and he <u>charged</u> Solomon his son, <u>saying</u>: "I go the way of all the earth; be strong, therefore, and <u>prove</u> yourself a man. And <u>keep</u> the charge of the LORD your God: to <u>walk</u> in His ways, to keep His statutes, His commandments, His judgments, and His testimonies, as it is written in the Law of Moses, that <u>you may prosper</u> in <u>all</u> that <u>you do</u> and wherever you turn;"   —1 Kings 2:1–3 (NKJV) Emphasis added

(This verse sounds a lot like the blessings of Psalm 1:3. "And whatever he does shall prosper.")

Please comment on David's and God's commands, warnings, and promises for smart choices and optimal life in 1 Kings 2:1–3. Notice the underlined action words and other relevant words that provide clues for what you may underline or circle in the following pages.

_____

_____

_____

_____

1. After having read the above verses, I believe I should:

_____

_____

_____

Please read the following Scriptures and underline or circle the action and other essential words.

> Commit your way to the LORD,
> Trust also in Him,
> And He shall bring *it* to pass.
> —Psalm 37:5 (NKJV)

> Trust in the LORD with all your heart,
> And lean not on your own understanding; In all your ways
> acknowledge Him,
> And He shall direct your paths.
> —Proverbs 3:5–6 (NKJV)

Finish what you start.

> Better is the end of a thing than the beginning thereof; *and* the patient in spirit is better than the proud in spirit..
> —Ecclesiastes 7:8 (ASV)

2. After having read the above verses, I think God wants me to:

_____

_____

_____

_____

_____

_____

> Your ears shall hear a word behind you, saying,
> "This *is* the way, walk in it,"
> Whenever you turn to the right hand
> Or whenever you turn to the left.
> —Isaiah 30:21 (NKJV)

> Fear not, for I *am* with you;
> Be not dismayed, for I *am* your God.
> I will strengthen you,
> Yes, I will help you,
> I will uphold you with My righteous right hand.'
> —Isaiah 41:10 (NKJV)

> 'Call to Me, and I will answer you, and show you great and mighty things, which you do not know.'
> —Jeremiah 33:3 (NKJV)

3. After having read the above verses, I believe God will help me to:

_____

_____

> For thus says the LORD: After seventy years are completed at Babylon, I will visit you and perform My good word toward you, and cause you to return to this place.
> —Jeremiah 29:10 (NKJV)

> And when you pray, do not use vain repetitions as the heathen *do.* For they think that they will be heard for their many words.
> "Therefore do not be like them. For your Father knows the things you have need of before you ask Him."
> —Matthew 6:7–8 (NKJV)

4. After having read the above verses, I believe the LORD will:

_____

_____

_____

> And Jesus came and spoke to them, saying, "All authority has been given to Me in heaven and on earth. Go therefore and make disciples of all the nations, baptizing them in the name of the Father and of the Son and of the Holy Spirit, teaching them to observe all things that I have commanded you; and lo, I am with you always, *even* to the end of the age." Amen.
> —Matthew 28:18–20 (NKJV)

5. After having read the above verse, I think Jesus wants me to:

_____

_____

_____

> For the love of money is a root of all *kinds of* evil, for which some have strayed from the faith in their greediness, and pierced themselves through with many sorrows. But you, O man of God, flee these things and pursue righteousness, godliness, faith, love, patience, gentleness. Fight the good fight of faith, lay hold on eternal life, to which you were also called and have confessed the good confession in the presence of many witnesses.
> — 1Timothy 6:10–12 (NKJV)

6. After reading the above verses, I believe, Father God wants me to:

_____

_____

_____

> And that servant, who knew his lord's will, and made not ready, nor did according to his will, shall be beaten with many *stripes;* —Luke 12:47 (ASV)

7. After having read the above verse, I think Father God wants me to:

_____

_____

> But the Helper, the Holy Spirit, whom the Father will send in My name, He will teach you all things, and bring to your remembrance all things that I said to you. —John 14:26 (NKJV)

> Now may He who supplies seed to the sower, and bread for food, supply and multiply the seed you have *sown* and increase the fruits of your righteousness,
> —2 Corinthians 9:10 (NKJV)

Father God will give you abundant finances to invest in His Kingdom. He will provide bread (food) for your physical needs. He will also increase your spiritual fruit: love, joy, peace, long-suffering, kindness, goodness, faithfulness, gentleness, self-control. (Galatians 5:22–23).

8. After having read the above verses, I believe the LORD will:

_____

_____

Understood

_____True, _____False:

Now that I understand the LORD'S will more perfectly, I am confident that He wants me to make the following changes in my life.

1. I believe Father God wants me to start:

    A. _____

    _____

    B. _____

    _____

    C. _____

    _____

2. I believe Father God wants and will help me to stop or finish:

    A. _____

    _____

    B. _____

    _____

    C. _____

    _____

3. I believe Father God wants and will help me to change or adjust my involvement with or in:

    A. _____

    _____

    B. _____

    _____

    C. _____

    _____

4. I believe Father God wants and will help me to spend more time with/at/on or doing:

    A. _____

    _____

    B. _____

    _____

    C. _____

    _____

5. I believe Father God wants and will help me to spend less time with, at, or on:

    A. _____

    _____

    B. _____

    _____

    C. _____

    _____

And now, Dear Reader, Father God is ready to help you to adjust your desires and set some wholesome goals that will be more pleasing[17] to Him and to you. The following prayer may help to start the process.

Dear Heavenly Father,

I ask for Your wisdom, grace, and guidance to establish and follow through on my plans. And if I happen to become hesitant or overzealous regarding any of these commitments, please strengthen my faith and self-control to change any or all of them as Your Spirit leads.

P.S:

_____
_____
_____
_____
_____

Amen.

Name:_____

Date/Time:_____

Comments:

_____
_____
_____
_____
_____
_____

If you would like to speak with a prayer minister, who will listen and pray for you, call the
**Hope Connection
718-238-4600**.

The Appendix has Sample Forms for writing your goals.

---

[17] Donation Ncb - New Cote Brilliante Church Of God, https://www.newcbcog.org/donation-ncb/ (accessed September 01, 2018).

Note: Reading C. Peter Wagner's book, *Your Spiritual Gifts Can Help Your Church Grow,* may help you to identify which of God's spiritual gifts are most operational in your life. Knowing your gifting may help you to set personal, ministry, and professional goals that are in harmony with your spiritual gifts.

Free Spiritual Gifts Quiz!

To identify your spiritual gifts, please download the FREE *Wagner-Modified Houts Questionnaire;* just type or copy and paste or type the following link to your browser to download a FREE Spiritual Gifts Questionnaire/Score Sheet with 125 questions) in PDF format: http://www.firstchristiantemple.or g/wpcontent/uploads/wagner_mo dified_houts.pdf

Prepare yourself to serve God by Memorizing His Word!

Next, you are invited to invest your time wisely to equip yourself to serve God. He will be delighted to release His amazing blessings that will flow through you—when you understand, memorize, and rightly apply His Word, and are ready to share His message with others as the Holy Spirit leads.

* * *

"Your word *is* a lamp to my feet
And a light to my path" (Psalm 119:105 (NKJV)).

10

Want to Please God? Memorize His Word!

Delight the Lord, and surprise your pastor, family, and friends by reciting Bible verses that you have memorized! If God has blessed you with some free time, why not use it to learn His Powerful Word that will strengthen you to help others and transform you into a ready spiritual dynamo?

The fact that you have arrived at this point in the book shows God has His eye on you and has already begun a good work in you. If you had no desire for the things of God—you would have stopped reading long before now, but here you are, all bright-eyed and hungry for more!

It is time to keep moving with God and let Him groom you with His Word to become a spiritual champ-

ion. He has exciting victories planned for you that might even cause King David "The Giant-Killer" to peek through Heaven's windows and wish (if it were possible) that you had been among his famous mighty men.

The secret to effective Scripture memorization is to understand each verse's meaning, why God said it, and to whom He was speaking. What was the need then and now? What did He want to happen then, and how does He want you to rightly apply His Word for yourself and others who need His help.

After memorizing a verse of Scripture, review the passage often to quote it accurately and freely as the Holy Spirit leads. When God's Word is in you, He will undoubtedly bring it through you! Nobody told me years ago when I was learning to memorize Bible verses, that God would be scheduling *divine appointments* for me to share those same passages (that are spirit and life) to bless others. If I had known how He would anoint and use them, and what great blessings and joy they would bring, I would certainly have memorized a whole lot more!

Expect glorious and exciting adventures with God because Jesus will be working with you, year-after-year, confirming His Living Word with signs following, according to Mark 16:20—not just for now, but for the rest of your life. This is why

— By Mary A. Bruno, Ph.D.

we must think in terms of a lifetime promise to serve God, with no room for turning back. Life keeps getting more joyful and exciting as we continue to walk with God.

When the Holy Spirit causes God's living Word to well up and flow through you at the right time, in the right place, and for the right reasons, you will become a walking powerhouse for Him! The Lord will lead you, fill you with His love and power, and help you to do the following, and more.

- Bring a word in season to those who are weary;

- Set captives free;

- Help others to receive Jesus, the Christ/Messiah, as Savior;

- Rebuke the enemy and watch him flee;

- Lay hands on the sick and see them recover;

- Speak peace that calms troubled situations;

- Pray God's Word and claim His promises;

- Lift up the downtrodden;

- Command evil spirits to leave, and they will go.

- Bring hope and peace that glorifies God.

Why not meet with a friend, or a group of friends, and commit the following Bible verses to memory—one verse at a time? It will be fun, and Jesus will be there to participate and help. He said in John 6:63, "It is the Spirit who gives life; the flesh profits nothing. The words that I speak to you are spirit, and *they* are life." When Spirit and life flow into you, guess what flows out from you—Spirit and life!

Scripture Memorization

Challenge yourself to memorize Scripture.

You can do this!

Please, date and initial each Bible passage—when you can recite it correctly from memory.

Now let's get started on learning God's Word.

1. Pause and think about what each verse means.

2. To whom it was addressed.

3. Why God said it

4. What was the need?

5. How God wants you to share it.

6. Expect Jesus to confirm His Word—that is alive and sharper than any two-edged sword.

Remember, as you share these encouraging passages, the LORD will be working with you and confirming His Word with signs following. Some of which you may recognize, and others may remain His personal work in the heart of the hearer(s).

Memorize the message (verse), speaking with love, understanding, and compassion, as though God were using you to bring His Word to help yourself and others. Avoid blurting out Scripture like a bunch of mindless words that were merely memorized to earn extra points.

Try saying John 3:16 in compassionate and meaningful phrases that convey what is on God's heart, as if He were speaking directly and tenderly through you to help someone. Think of the sharing of each Scripture passage as if you were throwing a life-preserver to a drowning person.

> For God so loved the world that He gave His only begotten Son, that whoever believes in Him should not perish but have everlasting life.
> —John 3:16 (NKJV)

Again, let this be your guide to learning God's precious Word. Memorize the message. Speak one phrase at a time with love, understanding, mercy, and kindness.

Father God will be scheduling *divine appointments* for you. Count on it, not only for right now but throughout your lifetime. Each memorized verse may become like a time-released breakthrough missile of life and hope that will well-up within your spirit as needed.

Being ready for Father God to use you involves more than quoting His Word; it includes walking uprightly with a pure heart and no secret sin or compromise. As you would serve a beautiful meal on a spotless plate, God wants to serve His spiritual feast on a clean heart.

> Depart! Depart! Go out from there,
> Touch no unclean *thing;*
> Go out from the midst of her,
> Be clean,
> You who bear the vessels of
> the LORD.   —Isaiah 52:11 (NKJV)

What kind of memory goals will you set? One, two, or three verses a day? One every other day? Four verses per week? Remember to write down your memorization goal and stick with it. After a week or so, feel free to adjust your plan according to your ability.

Expect to be tested. The enemy fears the power of God's Word that a believer can use to defeat him in a heartbeat. He will try to discourage or divert you from reaching your goal. On the other hand, Father God sees your dedication, and He is already transforming *you* into a spiritual Sword-wielding (Scripture-wielding), devil-defeating, God-honoring, soul-winning, Bible-believing victorious champion in His kingdom.

Learning Scripture brings eternal rewards. As you know, the secret to good Bible memorization is to understand the meaning and how to apply it well for yourself and others. These selected Bible verses will become like close friends. Be sure to learn their addresses (chapter and verse) so that you can revisit them as needed.

Heavenly High-Five Shouts!

Want to make Jesus smile when thinking of you? Try this. After memorizing each verse or set of verses, pause, raise both hands high toward heaven and give Him a *Heavenly High-Five* (Shout five "Hallelujahs" one after the other!) It will be fun, bless the LORD, chase the blues away, renew your strength, and make you feel terrific.

Important! A wise person will pray the following verse every time—before reading or trying to memorize Scripture,

> Open my eyes, that I may see Wondrous things from Your law.
>
> —Psalm 119:18 (NKJV)

Review your Bible verses often so you can quote them correctly as the Holy Spirit leads. When God's Word is in you, count on Him to bring it through you with a burst of His Holy Spirit Fire and Power!

Memorizing Scripture will change you forever. Father God will be pleased because—you will have become like His fully-stocked walking spiritual pantry, from which He can draw out the makings for a spiritual feast, a word in season, etc., whenever there is a need. The Holy Spirit will be present with His glorious Fire from On High, and of course, Jesus will be there with you and will confirm His Word.

You will have become a champion by learning the **100 Bible Verses** and will be ready to *tackle whole chapters and whole books of the Bible.* Doing so will distinguish you from the rest of the crowd. It will help to strengthen your confidence, deepen your love and knowledge of Jesus, better equip you to minister to others, and *accomplish great exploits* for God. Pause and think about all God will be able to do through you!

> But as it is written:
> "**Eye has not seen**, nor ear heard, Nor have entered into the heart of man The things which God **has** prepared for those who love Him." —1 Corinthians 2:9 (NKJV)

Comments:

_____

_____

_____

_____

Suggested chapters and books to memorize from the NKJV —after you have memorized all of the 100

Bible Verses that start on the following page.

Please consider these chapters and books and memorize your favorites:

Palm 91   Date memorized: _____

1 Corinthians 13

Date memorized: _____

1 John 1   Date memorized: _____

1 John 2   Date memorized: _____

1 John 3   Date memorized: _____

1 John 4   Date memorized: _____

1 John 5   Date memorized: _____

2 John   Date memorized: _____

3 John   Date memorized: _____

Jude   Date memorized: _____

James 1   Date memorized: _____

James 2   Date memorized: _____

James 3   Date memorized: _____

James 4   Date memorized: _____

James 5   Date memorized: _____

1Peter 1   Date memorized: _____

1 Peter 2 Date memorized: _____

1 Peter 3 Date memorized: _____

1 Peter 4 Date memorized: _____

1 Peter 5 Date memorized: _____

2 Peter 1 Date memorized: _____

2 Peter 2 Date memorized: _____

2 Peter 3 Date memorized: _____

> But the people that know their God shall be strong, and do *exploits*.
> —Daniel 11:32b (ASV)

100 Bible Verses

Start now to memorize all 100 of the following Bible verses!

(New King James Version®. Copyright © 1982 by Thomas Nelson.)

Psalm 1:1–6 (NKJV)

1 Blessed *is* the man
Who walks not in the counsel of the ungodly,
Nor stands in the path of sinners,
Nor sits in the seat of the scornful;
2 But his delight *is* in the law of the LORD,
And in His law he meditates day and night.
3 He shall be like a tree
Planted by the rivers of water,
That brings forth its fruit in its season,
Whose leaf also shall not wither;
And whatever he does shall prosper.

4 The ungodly *are* not so,
But *are* like the chaff which the wind drives away.
5 Therefore the ungodly shall not stand in the judgment,
Nor sinners in the congregation of the righteous.

6 For the LORD knows the way of the righteous,
But the way of the ungodly shall perish.

Date memorized: _____

Psalm 37:4 (NKJV)

4 Delight yourself also in the LORD,
And He shall give you the desires of your heart.

Date memorized: _____

Psalm 84:11 (NKJV)

For the LORD God *is* a sun and shield;
The LORD will give grace and glory;
No good *thing* will He withhold
From those who walk uprightly.

Date memorized: _____

Proverbs 3:5–6 (NKJV)

5 Trust in the LORD with all your heart,
And lean not on your own understanding;
6 In all your ways acknowledge Him,
And He shall direct your paths.

Date memorized: _____

Proverbs 14:12 (NKJV)

12 There is a way *that seems* right to a man,
But its end *is* the way of death.

Date memorized: _____

Proverbs 16:7 (NKJV)

When a man's ways please the LORD,
He makes even his enemies to be at peace with him.

Date memorized: _____

Proverbs 22:24–25 (NKJV)

24 Make no friendship with an angry man,
And with a furious man do not go,
25 Lest you learn his ways
And set a snare for your soul.

Date memorized: _____

Isaiah 30:21 (NKJV)

21 Your ears shall hear a word behind you, saying,
"This *is* the way, walk in it,"

Whenever you turn to the right hand
Or whenever you turn to the left.

Date memorized: _____

Isaiah 41:10 (NKJV)
[10] Fear not, for I *am* with you;
Be not dismayed, for I *am* your God.
I will strengthen you,
Yes, I will help you,
I will uphold you with My righteous right
hand.'

Date memorized: _____

Isaiah 55:8–9 (NKJV)
[8] "For My thoughts *are* not your
thoughts,
Nor *are* your ways My ways," says
the LORD.
[9] "For *as* the heavens are higher than the
earth,
So are My ways higher than your ways,
And My thoughts than your thoughts."

Date memorized: _____

Isaiah 55:10–11 (NKJV)
[10] "For as the rain comes down, and the
snow from heaven,
And do not return there,
But water the earth,
And make it bring forth and bud,
That it may give seed to the sower
And bread to the eater,
[11] So shall My word be that goes forth
from My mouth;
It shall not return to Me void,
But it shall accomplish what I please,
And it shall prosper *in the thing* for
which I sent it."

Date memorized: _____

Isaiah 65:24 (NKJV)
[24] "It shall come to pass
That before they call, I will answer;
And while they are still speaking, I
will hear."

Date memorized: _____

Jeremiah 29:11 (NKJV)
[11] For I know the thoughts that I think
toward you, says the LORD, thoughts of
peace and not of evil, to give you a
future and a hope.

Date memorized: _____

Malachi 3:10 (NKJV)
[10] "Bring all the tithes into
the storehouse,
That there may be food in My house,
And try Me now in this,"
Says the LORD of hosts,
"If I will not open for you the windows of
heaven
And pour out for you *such* blessing
That *there will* not *be room* enough *to
receive it.*"

Date memorized: _____

Matthew 6:9–13 (NKJV)
[9] In this manner, therefore, pray:
Our Father in heaven,
Hallowed be Your name.
[10] Your kingdom come.
Your will be done
On earth as *it is* in heaven.
[11] Give us this day our daily bread.
[12] And forgive us our debts,
As we forgive our debtors.
[13] And do not lead us into temptation,
But deliver us from the evil one.
For Yours is the kingdom and the power

and the glory forever. Amen.

Date memorized: _____

Matthew 6:14–15 (NKJV)
14 "For if you forgive men their trespasses, your heavenly Father will also forgive you. 15 But if you do not forgive men their trespasses, neither will your Father forgive your trespasses."

Date memorized: _____

Matthew 7:1–2 (NKJV)
"Judge not, that you be not judged. 2 For with what judgment you judge, you will be judged; and with the measure you use, it will be measured back to you."

Date memorized: _____

Matthew 18:18–19 (NKJV)
18 "Assuredly, I say to you, whatever you bind on earth will be bound in heaven, and whatever you loose on earth will be loosed in heaven.
19 "Again I say to you that if two of you agree on earth concerning anything that they ask, it will be done for them by My Father in heaven."

Date memorized: _____

Matthew 28:18–20 (NKJV)
18 And Jesus came and spoke to them, saying, "All authority has been given to Me in heaven and on earth.
19 Go therefore and make disciples of all the nations, baptizing them in the name of the Father and of the Son and of the Holy Spirit, 20 teaching them to observe all things that I have commanded you;

and lo, I am with you always, *even* to the end of the age." Amen.

Date memorized: _____

Mark 3:25 (NKJV)
25 "And if a house is divided against itself, that house cannot stand."

Date memorized: _____

Mark 4:22 (NKJV)
22 "For there is nothing hidden which will not be revealed, nor has anything been kept secret but that it should come to light."

Date memorized: _____

Mark 10:27 (NKJV)
27 But Jesus looked at them and said, "With men *it is* impossible, but not with God; for with God all things are possible."

Date memorized: _____

Mark 11:23 (NKJV)
23 "For assuredly, I say to you, whoever says to this mountain, 'Be removed and be cast into the sea,' and does not doubt in his heart, but believes that those things he says will be done, he will have whatever he says."

Date memorized: _____

Mark 16:20 (NKJV)
20 And they went out and preached everywhere, the Lord working with *them* and confirming the word through the accompanying signs. Amen.

Date memorized: _____

Luke 4:18–19 (NKJV)

18 "The Spirit of the L ORD *is* upon Me,
Because He has anointed Me
To preach the gospel to *the* poor;
He has sent Me to heal the
brokenhearted,
To proclaim liberty to *the* captives
And recovery of sight to *the* blind,
To set at liberty those who
are oppressed;
19 To proclaim the acceptable year of
the L ORD."

Date memorized: _____

Luke 6:38 (NKJV)

38 "Give, and it will be given to you: good
measure, pressed down, shaken
together, and running over will be put
into your bosom. For with the same
measure that you use, it will be
measured back to you."

Date memorized: _____

Luke 10:27b (NKJV)

'You shall love the L ORD your God with
all your heart, with all your soul, with all
your strength, and with all your mind,'
and 'your neighbor as yourself.' "

Date memorized: _____

John 1:12 (NKJV)

12 But as many as received Him, to them
He gave the right to become children of
God, to those who believe in His name:

Date memorized: _____

John 3:16–17 (NKJV)

16 For God so loved the world that He
gave His only begotten Son, that
whoever believes in Him should not
perish but have everlasting life. **17** For
God did not send His Son into the world
to condemn the world, but that the
world through Him might be saved.

Date memorized: _____

John 6:63 (NKJV)

63 It is the Spirit who gives life; the flesh
profits nothing. The words that I speak
to you are spirit, and *they* are life.

Date memorized: _____

John 14:6 (NKJV)

6 Jesus said to him, "I am the way, the
truth, and the life. No one comes to the
Father except through Me."

Date memorized: _____

John 14:26 (NKJV)

26 But the Helper, the Holy Spirit, whom
the Father will send in My name, He will
teach you all things, and bring to
your remembrance all things that I said
to you.

Date memorized: _____

John 13:34–35 (NKJV)

34 "A new commandment I give to you,
that you love one another; as I have
loved you, that you also love one
another. **35** By this all will know that you
are My disciples, if you have love for one
another."

Date memorized: _____

John 15:16 (NKJV)

[16] You did not choose Me, but I chose you and appointed you that you should go and bear fruit, and *that* your fruit should remain, that whatever you ask the Father in My name He may give you.

Date memorized: _____

Acts 1:8 (NKJV)

[8] "But you shall receive power when the Holy Spirit has come upon you; and you shall be witnesses to Me in Jerusalem, and in all Judea and Samaria, and to the end of the earth."

Date memorized: _____

Romans 3:23 (NKJV)

[23] For all have sinned and fall short of the glory of God,

Date memorized: _____

Romans 10:9–10 (NKJV)

[9] that if you confess with your mouth the Lord Jesus and believe in your heart that God has raised Him from the dead, you will be saved. [10] For with the heart one believes unto righteousness, and with the mouth confession is made unto salvation.

Date memorized: _____

1 Corinthians 10:13 (NKJV)

[13] No temptation has overtaken you except such as is common to man; but God *is* faithful, who will not allow you to be tempted beyond what you are able, but with the temptation will also make the way of escape, that you may be able to bear *it.*

Date memorized: _____

2 Corinthians 5:17 (NKJV)

[17] Therefore, if anyone *is* in Christ, *he is* a new creation; old things have passed away; behold, all things have become new.

Date memorized: _____

2 Corinthians 6:2 (NKJV)

[2] For He says:
"In an acceptable time I have heard you,
And in the day of salvation I have helped you."
Behold, now *is* the accepted time; behold, now *is* the day of salvation.

Date memorized: _____

2 Corinthians 6:14 (NKJV)

[14] Do not be unequally yoked together with unbelievers. For what fellowship has righteousness with lawlessness? And what communion has light with darkness?

Date memorized: _____

2 Corinthians 10:3–5 (NKJV)

[3] For though we walk in the flesh, we do not war according to the flesh. [4] For the weapons of our warfare *are* not carnal but mighty in God for pulling down strongholds, [5] casting down arguments and every high thing that exalts itself against the knowledge of God, bringing every thought into captivity to the obedience of Christ,

Date memorized: _____

Choices & Strongholds

— By Mary A. Bruno, Ph.D.

2 Timothy 2:15 (NKJV)

[15] Be diligent to present yourself approved to God, a worker who does not need to be ashamed, rightly dividing the word of truth.

Date memorized: _____

2 Timothy 3:1–7 (NKJV)

But know this, that in the last days perilous times will come: [2] For men will be lovers of themselves, lovers of money, boasters, proud, blasphemers, disobedient to parents, unthankful, unholy, [3] unloving, unforgiving, slanderers, without self-control, brutal, despisers of good, [4] traitors, headstrong, haughty, lovers of pleasure rather than lovers of God, [5] having a form of godliness but denying its power. And from such people turn away! [6] For of this sort are those who creep into households and make captives of gullible women loaded down with sins, led away by various lusts, [7] always learning and never able to come to the knowledge of the truth.

Date memorized: _____

Galatians 5:16 (NKJV)

[16] I say then: Walk in the Spirit, and you shall not fulfill the lust of the flesh.

Date memorized: _____

Galatians 5:19–21 (NKJV)

[19] Now the works of the flesh are evident, which are: adultery, fornication, uncleanness, lewdness, [20] idolatry, sorcery, hatred, contentions, jealousies, outbursts of wrath, selfish ambitions, dissensions, heresies, [21] envy, murders, drunkenness, revelries, and the like; of which I tell you beforehand, just as I also told *you* in time past, that those who practice such things will not inherit the kingdom of God.

Date memorized: _____

Galatians 5:22–25 (NKJV)

[22] But the fruit of the Spirit is love, joy, peace, longsuffering, kindness, goodness, faithfulness, [23] gentleness, self-control. Against such there is no law. [24] And those *who are* Christ's have crucified the flesh with its passions and desires. [25] If we live in the Spirit, let us also walk in the Spirit.

Date memorized: _____

Galatians 6:9 (NKJV)

[9] And let us not grow weary while doing good, for in due season we shall reap if we do not lose heart.

Date memorized: _____

Ephesians 2:8–9 (NKJV)

[8] For by grace you have been saved through faith, and that not of yourselves; *it is* the gift of God, [9] not of works, lest anyone should boast.

Date memorized: _____

Philippians 4:8 (NKJV)

[8] Finally, brethren, whatever things are true, whatever things *are* noble, whatever things *are* just, whatever things *are* pure, whatever things *are* lovely, whatever things *are* of good report, if *there is* any virtue and if *there is* anything praiseworthy—meditate on these things.

— By Mary A. Bruno, Ph.D.

Date memorized: _____

Philippians 4:13 (NKJV)

[13] I can do all things through Christ who strengthens me.

Date memorized: _____

Colossians 3:17 (NKJV)

[17] And whatever you do in word or deed, *do* all in the name of the Lord Jesus, giving thanks to God the Father through Him.

Date memorized: _____

James 1:5–8 (NKJV)

[5] If any of you lacks wisdom, let him ask of God, who gives to all liberally and without reproach, and it will be given to him. [6] But let him ask in faith, with no doubting, for he who doubts is like a wave of the sea driven and tossed by the wind. [7] For let not that man suppose that he will receive anything from the Lord; [8] *he is* a double-minded man, unstable in all his ways.

Date memorized: _____

James 1:12–15 (NKJV)

[12] Blessed *is* the man who endures temptation; for when he has been approved, he will receive the crown of life which the Lord has promised to those who love Him. [13] Let no one say when he is tempted, "I am tempted by God"; for God cannot be tempted by evil, nor does He Himself tempt anyone.

[14] But each one is tempted when he is drawn away by his own desires and enticed. [15] Then, when desire has conceived, it gives birth to sin; and sin, when it is full-grown, brings forth death.

Date memorized: _____

James 4:7–8 (NKJV)

[7] Therefore submit to God. Resist the devil and he will flee from you. [8] Draw near to God and He will draw near to you. Cleanse *your* hands, *you* sinners; and purify *your* hearts, *you* double-minded.

Date memorized: _____

1 John 1:9 (NKJV)

[9] If we confess our sins, He is faithful and just to forgive us *our* sins and to cleanse us from all unrighteousness.

Date memorized: _____

Revelation 3:5 (NKJV)

[5] He who overcomes shall be clothed in white garments, and I will not blot out his name from the Book of Life; but I will confess his name before My Father and before His angels.

Date memorized: _____

(Scriptures were taken from the *New King James Version*®. Copyright © 1982 by Thomas Nelson.)

Congratulations on your outstanding achievement!

Appendix

Samples Included:

- Completed Goals Form
- Blank Goals Form
- Year-End Goals Report

Sample: Seven Goals for 20_____

"Delight yourself also in the LORD, And He shall give you the desires of your heart" (Psalm 37:4 (NKJV)).

"Dear Lord,
I rely on You and ask for Your grace and provision to help me achieve these goals:"

1. Spiritual

Meet with God, read His Word daily. Attend weekly worship services. Memorize fifty-two (52) Bible verses each year.

To accomplish this, I will: *set the alarm for 15-30 minutes earlier, etc.*

2. Finish or Stop

Finish my degree. Stop wasting time.

To accomplish this, I will: *turn my assignments in on time.*

3. Educational, Self-Improvement

Mend relationship with Joe; keep my room neat. Save for a car.

To accomplish this, I will: *pray, and forgive, make the bed, get a job.*

4. Financial

Pay God's tithes and give my offerings.   Put 5-10% in savings acc.

To accomplish this, I will: *take God's tithe to my house of worship*

5. Professional and/or Ministry

Start or expand my business or ministry.

To accomplish this, I will: *Place an ad on social media this month.*

6. Avoid

Driving over the speed limit.

To achieve this, I will: *allow extra time to get to work, class, etc.*

7. Other

Share God's salvation message with at least 12 people this year.

To accomplish this, I will: *Pray, hand out tracts, follow God's lead.*

By Father God's grace and my diligent efforts, I will achieve all of these goals this year.

Signed: *Dedicated Child of God*   Date: *Today's date*

Choices & Strongholds   — By Mary A. Bruno, Ph.D.

*Seven Goals for 20*_____

"Delight yourself also in the LORD, And He shall give you the desires of your heart"
(Psalm 37:4 (NKJV)).

1. Spiritual: _____

To accomplish this, I will: _____

2. Finish, Stop: _____

To accomplish this, I will: _____

3. Educational, Self-Improvement: _____

To accomplish this, I will: _____

4. Financial: _____

To accomplish this, I will: _____

5. Professional and/or Ministry: _____

To accomplish this, I will: _____

6. Avoid: _____

To accomplish this, I will: _____

7. Other: _____

To accomplish this, I will: _____

Dear Lord,
I rely on You and am asking for Your grace and provision to help me reach these goals:" By Your grace and my efforts, I will achieve all of them this year.

Signed: _____ Date:_____

 Now that you have settled and documented your decisions and goals, God will help to bring them to pass. May His wisdom, understanding, and grace bring long-term guidance and victory as you continue to thrive in His perfect will.

Choices & Strongholds   — By Mary A. Bruno, Ph.D.

*Year-End Goals Report for 20*_____

Please comment on your goal progress to date.

1. Spiritual: _____

_____

_____

_____

2. Finish, Stop: _____

_____

_____

_____

3. Personal, Self-Improvement: _____

_____

_____

_____

4. Financial: _____

_____

_____

5. Professional and/or Ministry: _____

_____

_____

6. Avoid: _____

_____

_____

7. Other: _____

_____

Thank You, Lord, for the progress I have made toward my goals.

Signed: _____ Date:_____

Bibliography

Resources consulted during research for this book include the following:

Books

American Standard Version (ASV)
   Public Domain

Amplified Bible (AMP)
Copyright © 2015by The Lockman Foundation,
La Habra, CA 90631.
All rights reserved.

The Chicago Manual of Style, Sixteenth Edition.
Chicago: The University of Chicago Press, 2010.

Jubilee Bible 2000 (JUB)
Copyright © 2013, 2020
by Ransom Press International

The King James Version (KJV)
Public Domain.

New King James Version (NKJV)
Scripture taken from the New King James Version®. Copyright © 1982 by Thomas Nelson.
Used by permission. All rights reserved.

The New Strong's Exhaustive Concordance of the Bible
Strong, James, LL.D., S.T.D.
Nashville,
Thomas Nelson Publisher 1990

The Passion Translation (TPT)
The Passion®. Copyright © 2017 by BroadStreet Publishing® Group, LLC.
Used by permission.
All rights reserved.
thepassiontranslation.com

Websites Contacted
BibleGateway
https://www.biblegateway.com/

BlueLetterBible.org
https://www.blueletterbible.org/

(Wagner Modified Houts Questionnaire, at Charles E.Fuller Institute of Evangelism and Church Growth, Pasadena, CA)
http://www.firstchristiantemple.org/w-content/uploads/wagner_modified_houts.pdf

THE END (Book One)

BOOK: TWO

Dare to Pull Down Strongholds!

Now is the Time!

(Updated 04/25/2021)

By

Mary A. Bruno, Ph.D.

V447- 669X961-13pt -122018-082319—154

Mary A. Bruno, Ph.D.,

author, and ordained minister, serves with her husband, the Reverend, Doctor Rocco Bruno. She is Co-founder and Vice-President of Interdenominational Ministries International, and Co-founder/Vice-Chancellor of IMI Bible College & Seminary in Vista, California. She has earned a Ministerial Diploma from LIFE Bible College; a Master of Theology, and a Doctor of Ministry Degree from the School of Bible Theology, which awarded her the Honorary Doctor of Divinity Degree. She earned a Doctor of Theology Degree from IMI Bible College & Seminary; and a Doctor of Philosophy Degree in Pastoral Christian Counseling from Evangelical Theological Seminary.

Her talks include humor, witty insights, and Scripture. She has ministered in the USA and abroad. Turnouts skyrocketed when she presided over the Vista Women's Aglow. Her "Words in Season" radio broadcast aired in the 1980s and '90s over KPRZ and KCEO in San Diego County. Watch for her next book release at www.amazon.com. Visit her website at www.ministrylit.com.

For Speaking Engagements:
Email: imibcs@aol.com
Or write: **Dr. Mary A. Bruno**
P.O. Box 2107
Vista, California 92085
United States of America

Publication Date: December 20, 2018

Printed in the United States of America

Mary A. Bruno, Vista, California, December 2018

International Standard Book Number ISBN: 9781790877393

978-0-9976681-2-4

BISAC Category: RELO12040
Religion/ Christian Life/ Spiritual Warfare

BISAC Category: RELO12040
Religion/Christian Life/General

Library of Congress Control Number: 2018914791

Mary A. Bruno, Vista, CA

[V-447-122018/082319/154P]

To our sweet memories of the Reverend Florence A. Parker, D.D., my Mother. Her diligent service to God with her time and talents often put younger generations to shame.

Doctor Parker was one of God's high-ranking "behind the scenes" soldiers of the faith. Her decades of consistent prayer and financial support secretly helped numerous ministers, missionaries, and ministries to hold their positions on the battlefront and fulfill their God-given callings.

As Professor of the IMI Bible College & Seminary's Ministries Department, she did not waiver when mounds of theses and dissertations arrived for review. She just smiled, adjusted her gold-rimmed glasses, sat at her desk, and carefully examined every word.

Her faithful service, encouragement, and faith will be cherished and long remembered by all who were blessed to have known her.

Mary

Foreword

In this book Dr. Bruno has managed to hit the soft spot, the place that we find lacking in life.

We pray; we seek God, we go to church, and hopefully read our Bibles, but what is it that is lacking? After reading her manuscript, I can see how God has so much more for me, and I believe you will feel the same for yourself. There are areas in life that we need to address, plus areas that show us we are doing things right.

What an Amazing God we serve! He has provided every means possible for us to learn, to grow, and to find our destiny in Him.

Dr. Bruno clearly points out that it is up to us to follow Father God's lead and press ahead with His Word and His commands.

My prayer for you is that as you read these anointed and powerful words, you will gain a new understanding of what God wants for you in your life and in your relationship with Him.

Rev. Dr. Barbara A. Yovino,

Associate Pastor at Gateway City Church, in Brooklyn, NY; New York State Coordinator for the Day to Pray for the Peace of Jerusalem; New York Director of God.tv Prayer Line; Advisor to IMI Bible College & Seminary, and Vice-Pres./Director of the Christian Hope Network, in Brooklyn, NY. Prayer Line: 718-238-4600, www.chn.cc.

Visit Dr. Barbara A. Yovino and CHN on Facebook!

Acknowledgments

Special thanks to God's generous people who have helped make this book a reality, especially the Reverend Doctor Rocco Bruno, my multitalented, tri-lingual husband, a man of God, and missionary to Italy. His steady support is my treasure in his humble earthen vessel.

Others who have shared editorial comments:

The Rev. Mary Anne Moyer, B.C.Ed., M.C.Ed.(can.) has been a faithful proofreader and ready help from the beginning.

Jimmy Maynor, The Witness, "Pulling Down Strongholds"[18]; Vol III, No.2; March 1983. His insightful two-page article greatly enriched the study of this subject.

The Reverend Barbara Anne Yovino, Ph.D., Vice-Pres./Dir. of the Christian Hope Network, in Brooklyn, NY; Associate Pastor at Gateway City Church, in Brooklyn; New York State Coordinator for the Day to Pray for the Peace of Jerusalem; New York Dir. of God.tv Prayer Line; and advisor to IMI Bible College & Seminary.

San Diego Christian Writers Guild (SDCWG), San Marcos chapter hosted by Barbara Waite, with Sandy Anderson, Joni Doyle, Jan Flickinger, and Pat Whistler, shared great suggestions and tips.

Other Writers—Blessings to the many gifted writers whose books and websites (listed in the bibliography) enhanced the research phase. Any errors or omissions were accidental and purely unintentional. May God reward each person's labor for His glory.

Mary A. Bruno. Ph.D.

Preface

This writing has been prepared in the hope that it might help God's servants to dare to exercise their God-given power and authority to set captives free. The information outlined in this document is the culmination of over a decade of research and study.

The author extends special recognition and appreciation to Jimmy Maynor for his "Pulling Down Strongholds"[19] article in THE WITNESS newsletter, Vol III, No 2, dated March 1983. His excellent work served as a springboard of inspiration that launched chapter eleven.

Scripture Translations Used:

The New King James Version (NKJV) is the primary source of Scripture unless otherwise shown.

---

[18] Jimmy Maynor, The Witness, "Pulling Down Strongholds"; Vol III, No.2; March 1983.

[19] Jimmy Maynor, The Witness, "Pulling Down Strongholds"; Vol III, No.2; March 1983.

> But you *are* a chosen generation, a royal priesthood, a holy nation, His own special people, that you may proclaim the praises of Him who called you out of darkness into His marvelous light; —1 Peter 2:9 (NKJV)

1
Chosen Generation

The realization that one is part of a "chosen generation" puts an end to any feelings of insignificance. But of whom is the chosen generation comprised? They have heard and obeyed God's call to come out of darkness into His marvelous light. They have discovered His great purpose and direction for their lives and have found new reasons for living. Many of the chosen generation began much like the man Jesus met in Mark and Luke's gospels. Little did they dream Jesus would prepare them to pull down strongholds.

> Now they came to Jericho. As He went out of Jericho with His disciples and a great multitude, blind Bartimaeus, the son of Timaeus, sat by the road begging. And when he heard that it was Jesus of Nazareth, he began to cry out and say, "Jesus, Son of David, have mercy on me!" Then many warned him to be quiet; but he cried out all the more, "Son of David, have mercy on me!" So Jesus stood still and commanded him to be called.
> Then they called the blind man, saying to him, "Be of good cheer. Rise, He is calling you." And throwing aside his garment, he rose and came to Jesus. So Jesus answered and said to him, "What do you want Me to do for you?"
> The blind man said to Him, "Rabboni, that I may receive my sight." Then Jesus said to him, "Go your way; your faith has made you well." And immediately he received his sight and followed Jesus on the road.
> —Mark 10:46–52 (NKJV)

Called from Darkness to Light

Bartimaeus was blind and feeling rather insignificant that day when Jesus passed by Jericho. Jericho was a pretty tough neighborhood where people had to look out for themselves, but to Bartimaeus, it was home.

— By Mary A. Bruno, Ph.D.

His begging barely brought in enough coins or scraps each day to meet his immediate needs. He often felt misunderstood, overlooked, and unimportant, as he did that day in his usual spot by the side of the road. He appreciated the bright sun that warmed his body but could not penetrate his cold world of walking darkness.

The crowd was alive with excitement when Jesus came on the scene. Jerichonians expected to see Him perform a miracle or to expound on some profound teaching. Bartimaeus had heard about Jesus, whom some claimed was the promised Messiah, and realized this might be his chance of a life-time! He ignored codes of behavior and shouted at the top of his voice, "Jesus, Son of David, have mercy on me!"

Bartimaeus's loud cries made onlookers uncomfortable. They told him to keep silent for the sake of others, but personal need demanded he call out to God for mercy, and that he do so immediately! Bartimaeus's heart raced as he raised his voice and wailed even louder.

Jesus heard the cry of hope from that soul in distress and called for Bartimaeus to come. Old "Bart's" adrenalin was flowing. Trembling with expectancy, he grabbed his walking stick, sprang to his feet, and stagger-groped his way toward the sound of Jesus's voice. All eyes were on Jesus, the Great Healer, and Bartimaeus, the noisy beggar.

Get to the Point!

In an instant, God would pass over side issues and ask a life-changing question that would bring everything into focus and become Bartimaeus' turning point.

What would Bartimaeus say to Jesus? Was he just in this for the thrill of a charismatic moment with Jesus, the Great Miracle Worker? Bartimaeus knew that, if Jesus healed him, he would have to give up his identity as a beggar, and the only security he knew (begging). Was he ready to follow Jesus and leave his old way of life (panhandling) behind? What did he truly want from God? What was his greatest need? Was it a bag of shekels? A house? Some clothes? A donkey? Free food? A caregiver? A girlfriend? His sight?

> So Jesus stood still and commanded him to be brought to Him. And when he had come near, He asked him, saying,
> "What do you want Me to do for you?"
> He said, "Lord, that I may receive my sight."   —Luke 18:40–41 (NKJV)

Bartimaeus went for all or nothing and blurted out, "Lord, that I might receive my sight."

Choices & Stronghold   — By Mary A. Bruno, Ph.D.

When Bartimaeus used the word, *Lord,* he could have been confessing; he believed Jesus was God, the Messiah, and that Jesus was able to do the impossible. Bartimaeus did not ask for general healing. He may have thought Jesus *could* do that, but he needed help to *receive* his special healing. He was very specific—"Lord, *that I may receive* my sight."

Note: The word *receive* is used three times in three verses (Luke 18:40–42), which indicates God wants us to focus on *receiving*. It is one thing to *believe*, and quite another to *receive*. Bartimaeus wanted God's help so that he could do both.

> Then Jesus said to him, "Receive your sight; your faith has made you well." And immediately he received his sight, and followed Him, glorifying God. And all the people, when they saw *it,* gave praise to God.
> —Luke 18:42–43 (NKJV)

Bartimaeus left all, including his favorite begging spot, and followed Jesus.

What About Us?

That was awesome for Bartimaeus back then, but what about us (possibly "blinded" ones) today? The future seems dim. People all around us are restricted and handicapped by emotional hurts and bitter memories. We struggle with physical and emotional addictions and afflictions. Immorality's consequences and circumstances leave multitudes physically and spiritually blind, or emotionally disabled. Our needs, apart from the light of God's Word and divine intervention, may never be met.

Down from God's Holy Throne of Grace resounds the precious assurance of sacred verse that echoes through the ages with bright hope for today.

> But you *are* a chosen generation, a royal priesthood, a holy nation, His own special people, that you may proclaim the praises of Him who called you out of darkness into His marvelous light; who once *were* not a people but *are* now the people of God, who had not obtained mercy but now have obtained mercy.
> —1 Peter 2:9–10 (NKJV)

God's redeemed know that when we were nothing, Jesus Christ, the Good Shepherd of humankind's straying souls, dared to find, redeem, and restore that which some thought had no value. God's mercy is unfailing, and His ears are listening for our call.

A Holy Nation

The chosen generation is a holy nation, called to a new kingdom and a new nationality. When one welcomes the LORD Jesus Christ as personal LORD and Savior, he or she gains new citizenship in heaven, with a new name, a new identity, and a new reputation. His or her

Choices & Strongholds

— By Mary A. Bruno, Ph.D.

natural birth may have been a surprise to the parents on earth; however, Father God not only knew all about each natural birth but planned for each person's spiritual rebirth. We have been born of the Holy Spirit into God's family. Jesus's blood has cleansed and washed away the guilt and stains of our vilest sins. His presence within us keeps us from falling and helps us to walk in holiness.

> Now to Him who is able to keep you from stumbling,
> And to present *you* faultless
> Before the presence of His glory with exceeding joy,   —Jude 1:24 (NKJV)

A Called Nation

The chosen generation is a called-out nation of committed believers who serve and glorify King Jesus.

Called to Praise God

We are called to proclaim God's praises. Let's take a peek at the meaning of *proclaim* in, 1 Peter 2:9.

Strong's word G1804– *exangello,* translated as *proclaim,* on blueletterbible.org, means:[20]

   I. to tell out or forth

   II. to declare abroad, divulge, publish

   III. to make known by praising or proclaiming, to celebrate.

Declaring God's praises is our calling! To worship Him, we must first lift our eyes from our needs, complaints, and resentments, and focus on God's greatness. Our lips must learn to proclaim God's good works and intervention on behalf of His people. As we focus on His faithfulness and tender mercies, our hearts will overflow with faith, hope, and joy in the revelation of Who God is.

Called Out of Darkness

Darkness in 1 Peter 2:9 implies:

   I. darkness
   A. of night darkness
   B. of darkened eyesight or blindness;

   II. metaphor
   A. of ignorance respecting divine things and human duties, and the accompanying ungodliness and immorality, together with their consequent misery in hell
   B. persons in whom darkness becomes visible and holds sway.

This *darkness* is from the **Greek word:** σκότος **skótos,** skot'-os; from the base of G4639; shadiness, i.e. obscurity (literally or figuratively):—darkness. [21]

God calls us to come "out of the darkness" —all the way out of darkness (and all the way into)— "His marvelous light." This requires a choice and a response.

Obedience to His call will break the power of former circumstances.

After one's God encounter, salvation (being born-again) is the next step in breaking free from all that would bind or hold one back from following the LORD.

Jesus calls and helps us to leave our old routines, habits, and ungodly associates, and move on with Him. He calls us to walk in His new and living way on honorable paths. He came to set us free and wants His people enslaved to nothing and no one. He calls us to enjoy His sweet freedom and abundant life.

As with Bartimaeus, living within the confines of darkness did have some benefits, but were they ever worth their high price?

Comments:

_____

_____

_____

[20]https://www.blueletterbible.org/lang/Lexicon/Lexicon.cfm?strongs=G1804&t=KJV

[21]https://www.blueletterbible.org/lang/Lexicon/Lexicon.cfm?strongs=G4655&t=KJV

Next, we explore how to receive God's glorious privileges and abundant provisions that will enable us to undo heavy burdens and set captives free.

✳ ✳ ✳

> So Jesus said to them again, "Peace to you! As the Father has sent Me, I also send you."
> And when He had said this, He breathed on *them,* and said to them, "Receive the Holy Spirit."
> —John 20:21–22 (NKJV)

2

Commissioned and Equipped

The chosen generation recognizes God's presence and hears His voice. In Luke 4:16–19, we read that Jesus entered the synagogue on the Sabbath day. When it was time to read the Scripture, they handed Him an ancient scroll with Esaias [Isaiah] the prophet's writings.

Jesus chose that precise moment to explain why the Holy Spirit was upon Him. It was because of God's holy anointing, that sacred consecration with the divine presence, power, and equipping to preach the good news of salvation, that prepared Jesus for His divine mission on earth.

> So He came to Nazareth, [that Nazareth] where He had been brought up, and He entered the synagogue, as was His custom on the Sabbath day. And He stood up to read.
>
> And there was handed to Him [the roll of] the book of the prophet Isaiah. He opened (unrolled) the book and found the place where it was written,
>
> The Spirit of the Lord [is] upon Me, because He has anointed Me [the Anointed One, the Messiah] to preach the good news (the Gospel) to the poor; He has sent Me to announce release to the captives and recovery of sight to the blind, to send forth as delivered those who are oppressed [who are downtrodden, bruised, crushed, and broken down by calamity],
>
> To proclaim the accepted *and* acceptable year of the Lord [the day when salvation and the free favors of God profusely abound].
> —Luke 4:16–19
> Amplified Bible, Classic Edition (AMPC)

That must have created quite a stir because every eye in the place fastened on Jesus. Imagine the power of God that must have swept through that assembly when they heard *Him* read! It may have been the same synagogue he attended while growing up. What a shocker it must have been. Nobody uttered a word. They were astonished by Jesus's divine presence and the impact of God's Living Word. Then, to emphasize His point, Jesus told them the Scripture was fulfilled in their ears—*that day*! They had seen and heard its fulfillment and were accountable for how they responded to God's Word.

> In the beginning was the Word, and the Word was with God, and the Word was God. The same was in the beginning with God. All things were made through him; and without him was not anything made that hath been made. In him was life; and the life was the light of men. And the light shineth in the darkness; and the darkness apprehended it not. —John 1:1–5 (ASV)

The World Cannot Understand

The gathering of friends and neighbors tried to figure it out. Jesus was supposed to be Joseph's son; wasn't he? But no mortal had ever spoken with such life and soul-trembling power. The people still did not realize Jesus was God's Son; therefore, their natural [unregenerate] minds could not receive the things of God, but they knew something had happened.

> But the natural man does not receive the things of the Spirit of God, for they are foolishness to him; nor can he know *them,* because they are spiritually discerned.
> —1 Corinthians 2:14 (NKJV)

His Sheep Know His Voice

Those who know Jesus as Savior and LORD, also recognize His voice.

> And when he brings out his own sheep, he goes before them; and the sheep follow him, for they know his voice. —John 10:4 (NKJV)

They are eager to hear the gospel and ready to share Christ's message of salvation, healing, restoration, deliverance, and purpose.

Believe and Receive

It is one thing to believe, and another to receive. You may hear God knocking at the door of your heart and calling, "May I come in?" It is quite another thing for you to acknowledge and answer God's call and *receive* Him into your life.

> Behold, I stand at the door and knock: if any man hear my voice and open the door, I will come in to him, and will sup with him, and he with me. —Revelation 3:20 (ASV)

While dining with Jesus, He may share juicy things of His Kingdom.

We need to receive and entrust ourselves entirely and *permanently* to Jesus—The Messiah—our One and only LORD and Savior. If you have not already done so, you may do so now. Jesus has been waiting to welcome you into His family and wants to hear you say aloud that you believe He is God's only begotten Son and that you are receiving Him as your LORD and Savior.

> But as **many as received him**, to them gave he the right to become children of God, even to them that believe on his name:—John 1:12 (ASV)
> Emphasis added

The following prayer will help you to get started, and then just continue in your own words. Only you can choose to turn from your sin, to God, and make room in your heart and life for Him. This is called repenting or turning around.

Prayer to Receive Jesus Christ

Dear LORD Jesus,

I believe You are God's only begotten Son, and that You died on the Cross to pay for my sins and make me part of Your family.

I confess I have sinned, and receive You as my Savior. Thank You for hearing and answering my prayer. I am forgiven and am a new member of your family.

Please fill me with Your Holy Spirit, and show me how to accomplish Your will for my life.

I give up my old ways and will live for You. I will tell others about You, study my Bible, and talk with You daily. I love You, LORD.   Amen.

On this date, (Select one)

____I asked, ___I re-asked,

___I refused to ask, Jesus Christ to be my LORD and Savior.

Name_____

Date/Time_____

Welcome to God's family and the Chosen Generation! After believing and receiving Jesus (The Messiah), you will enjoy a new connection with Him and stop feeling guilty about the wrong choices of your past. Jesus will have wiped your record clean and given you a *full pardon!* — while you were praying!

> Wherefore if any man is in Christ, he is a new creature: the old things are passed away; behold, they are become new.
> —2 Corinthians 5:17 (ASV)

Suddenly, because God is love and He lives within your heart, you will love everybody and want to be in Father God's house (church) every time the doors open. This is one of the signs that Jesus is in your life— He loves to be in His Father's house—and so will you. Sinful expressions and habits will suddenly feel very uncomfortable and inappropriate. Because you will have become God's child, you will love what He loves and hate what He hates.

Healed

The chosen generation receives healing. God's people have re-covered their spiritual sight from religious errors and have come out of spiritual darkness. They can see and receive God's truth with joy.

God heals broken hearts that were wounded by sorrows, losses, betrayals, and failures of ourselves or others. He heals and restores us to love, trust, and hope again.

God heals bruises. Bruises are those ugly places in the body that happen when someone or something comes hard against a person. Bruises and injuries hurt! An injured party may try to cover or hide the hurts with a forced smile for fear of being harmed again by someone who might get too close to a sensitive area. When Jesus heals our bruises, they stop hurting! He frees us from our old wound's pains and limitations.

Liberated

God has canceled our spiritual debts and forgiven all of our sins and failures. His chosen generation does not linger to grieve at the shore of God's sea of forgetfulness, with its dregs of humanity's failure, debt, and sin. Heartfelt assurance brings new vision and direction. They do not dwell on former uncleanness or failures but move forward in holiness and victory.

God's high and holy calling has no place for fellowship with rebels and workers of spiritual error, who gratify lusts of their flesh that corrupt and steal one's heart and soul. Mercy and freedom, with blessings, purpose, and joy are the lots of God's called-out ones.

Commissioned

They are ordered and equipped to overcome. Matthew's gospel speaks of when Jesus issued the chosen generation's assignment:

> And as you go, preach, saying, 'The kingdom of heaven is at hand.' Heal the sick, cleanse the lepers, raise the dead, cast out demons. Freely you have received, freely give.
> —Matthew 10:7–8 (NKJV)

Mark also wrote about what Jesus said when He issued the believer's commission:

> And He said to them, "Go into all the world and preach the gospel to every creature. He who believes and is baptized will be saved; but he who does not believe will be condemned. And these signs will follow those who believe: In My name they will cast out demons; they will speak with new tongues; they will take up serpents; and if they drink anything deadly, it will by no means hurt them; they will lay hands on the sick, and they will recover."
> —Mark 16:15–18 (NKJV)

To "drive out" (cast out) demons in the above passages implies a forceful command that tears out, casts off, and causes an entity to let go and *depart with haste*. The words *drive out,* involve a swift command

and response, rather than a long, drawn-out deliverance session. They also mean to extract something that was inserted into something else, possibly such as plucking out a bee's stinger from someone who was stung, or like ejecting an empty shotgun shell. (This reminded me of Jesus, the Good Shepherd of our souls, tenderly removing a hypodermic needle from an addict's arm, casting down addiction's power, and fully restoring the person to live a joyful and productive life.)

For further study of "cast out" (in Matthew, 7:22, 8:16, 8:31, 9:33, 10:1, 10:8, 12:24, 12:28, etc.), see Strong's word number G1544, *ekballō* at blueletterbible.com.[22]

The book of Acts tells of the supernatural ability believers receive when the Holy Spirit comes upon them—to empower them to become witnesses of Jesus—to speak boldly about Who He is, what He does, and what He will do.

> "But you shall receive power when the Holy Spirit has come upon you; and you shall be witnesses to Me in Jerusalem, and in all Judea and Samaria, and to the end of the earth."　　—Acts 1:8 (NKJV)

> When the Day of Pentecost had fully come, they were all with one accord in one place. And suddenly there came a sound from. . .

> . . . heaven, as of a rushing mighty wind, And it filled the whole house where they were sitting. Then there appeared to them divided tongues, as of fire, and *one* sat upon each of them. And they were all filled with the Holy Spirit and began to speak with other tongues, as the Spirit gave them utterance.
> 　　—Acts 2:1–4 (NKJV)

The promised Holy Spirit's power is for all believers. Yes, even God's handmaidens also get to prophesy—which includes preaching. See blueletterbible.com word study on *prophesy* from the Greek word number G4395 *prophēteuō*.[23]

> "to prophesy, to be a prophet, speak forth by divine inspirations, to predict
>
> A. to prophesy
> B. with the idea of foretelling future events pertaining esp. to the kingdom of God
> C. to utter forth, declare, a thing which can only be known by divine revelation
> D. to break forth under sudden impulse in lofty discourse or praise of the divine counsels
> E. under like prompting, to teach, refute, reprove, admonish, comfort others
> F. To act as a prophet, discharge the prophetic office."

> 'And it shall come to pass in the last days, says God,
> That I will pour out of My Spirit on all flesh; Your sons and your daughters shall prophesy, . . .'

> '... Your young men shall see visions,
> Your old men shall dream dreams.
> "And on My menservants and on My maidservants
> I will pour out My Spirit in those days;
> And they shall prophesy.'
> —Acts 2:17–18 (NKJV)

What did Father God send Jesus to do? Once again, we read,

> The Spirit of the Lord is upon me,
> Because he anointed me to preach good tidings to the poor:
> He hath sent me to proclaim release to the captives,
> And recovering of sight to the blind,
> To set at liberty them that are bruised,
> To proclaim the acceptable year of the Lord. —Luke 4:18–19 (ASV)

Commissioned to Do the Works

> So Jesus said to them again, "Peace to you! As the Father has sent Me, I also send you." And when He had said this, He breathed on *them,* and said to them, "Receive the Holy Spirit.
> —John 20:21–22 (NKJV)

Jesus has commissioned us to do the same kind of works that He did while in His physical body on earth. John's gospel confirms that Jesus anoints, appoints, and sends His dedicated followers with similar ministry and equipping to what He had while on earth. For more reading on this subject, see Mark 16:15–18, Acts 1:8, Acts 2:1–4, Acts 2:17,18, and John 15:12.

Scripture proves God has called for, and fully requires, each generation of believers to obey His marching orders. We are commissioned (ordered).

Commissioned to Preach

Believers are charged and equipped to preach the gospel (good news) everywhere. It is God's priceless message of Jesus's holy life, death, resurrection, redemption, reconciliation, and restoration to fellowship and divine favor—for all who will become God's favored ones.

Commissioned to Heal the Sick

Believers are authorized and equiped to heal the sick [in body, soul, and spirit]. Jesus, the Messiah, lived, died, and rose again. He is the total Savior, for the total human. We have healing in His name, by His stripes, and by His Word.

> But he was wounded for our transgressions, he was bruised for our iniquities: the chastisement of our peace was upon him; and with his stripes we are healed.
> All we like sheep have gone astray; we have turned every one to his own way; and the LORD hath laid on him the iniquity of us all.
> —Isaiah 53:5–6 (KJV)

> Who Himself bore our sins in His own body on the tree, that we, having died to sins, might live for righteousness—by whose stripes you were healed. —1 Peter 2:24 (NKJV)

Commissioned to Cleanse the Lepers

Believers are anointed, appointed, and equipped to cleanse the lepers [unclean ones]. Sin is compared to the horrible disease of leprosy because it is highly contagious, can spread quickly, and can devour others by the unclean influence of one sin-bent person to another.

But with, just, one touch of the Master's hand; that which made a man an outcast can no longer hold him. When Jesus comes, He breaks sin's power! He cleanses and transforms spiritual lepers into new creatures in Christ, with godly values, godly appetites, holy desires, and holy joy!

Commissioned to Deliver the Captives

Spiritual snipers who shoot God's wounded children have brought much suffering to Christ's body. Jesus, the Captain of our Salvation, has ordered His troops to go and deliver the captives.

When God's soldiers get shot down while lingering too long in the enemy's camp or while exploring his territory, they can be caught off-guard and taken captive.

Commissioned —

To Bring Them Back Alive

God wants us to bring back those who are missing in action, and the prisoners of war (backsliders). He sees their anguish and has ordered His troops to bring them out. The Bible, when speaking of Jesus, reminds us,

> But there is a friend *who* sticks closer than a brother.
> —Proverbs 18:24b (NKJV)

Father God is looking for that level of commitment from His troops. Can He count on you to bring the good news of His mercy and restoration, and to extend an uplifting hand of compassion to those who need His forgiveness and help?

Comments:

_____

_____

_____

_____

_____

_____

***

---

[22]https://www.blueletterbible.org/lang/Lexicon/Lexicon.cfm?strongs=G1544&t=KJV

[23]https://www.blueletterbible.org/lang/Lexicon/Lexicon.cfm?strongs=G4395&t=KJV

> And as you go, preach, saying, 'The kingdom of heaven is at hand.' Heal the sick, cleanse the lepers, raise the dead, cast out demons. Freely you have received, freely give.
>
> Matthew 10:7–8 (NKJV)

3
Raise the Dead

God expects believers to exercise their authority over the devil and to eject demons when and where they show up, to tear down strongholds, and set the captives free.

Commissioned to Eject Demons

Webster's New Collegiate Dictionary defines the word "eject" as follows:

[24] **1 a:** to drive out, esp. by physical force **b:** to evict from property **2:** to throw out or off from within <the empty cartridges> --ejectable. . .
Syn EJECT, EXPEL, OUST, EVICT, DISMISS *shared meaning element:* to drive or force out.

James reminds us to,

> Resist the devil and he will flee from you.   —James 4:7b (NKJV)

That's not so complicated. *We* *r*esist (stand against and oppose), and *he* flees! The steps are, one—we resist, and two—the devil flees. What is so hard about that?

Let's not have any of that, "Just one more time, one more glass, one more puff or one more snort, and then you really must go," kind of thinking.

Note: This is why tithing is so important. It strengthens us to honor God first instead of ourselves, which toughens our self-control for when we will need it to resist the enemy.

Know Your Target

First, recognize the enemy's doings.

Second, come against the activity and put up your most diligent, wholehearted, steady resistance.

Third, an evil spirit knows he has to go [when believers, finally, get around to evicting him]. That's when he must cease and desist whatever he was trying to do, dash out in terror, run sobbing to his boss, and report that you threw him out.

There is a time to say, "Enough is enough!" and exercise our God-given authority to resist, confront, and evict an unclean spirit. The chosen generation dares to trust God when it appears to be too late.

— By Mary A. Bruno, Ph.D.

After Jesus told His followers to raise the dead, did He ever tell anyone to stop doing so?

Commissioned to Raise the Dead

The LORD Jesus Christ's resurrection life is still greater than death's power. We have heard reports of people who had untimely deaths but returned to life, in direct answer to a believer's prayer.

Beloved Pet

One of the ministers at a church my husband and I attended in San Marcos, California, told about the time his family was traveling through the Arizona desert. He said their little dog ran onto the road, was struck by a passing vehicle, and died. Everyone was heart-broken when their beloved pet's little body became stiff.

The man and his family prayed and kept on praying until life rushed back in with such force that their dog woke up and dashed from one person to another, jumping, licking, and wiggling, as if to say, "God sent me back! I'm alive again! Thank you for holding on in prayer!" — Wiggle, wiggle, wiggle, lick, lick, lick! Joy tears washed away their tears of grief when God answered prayer for their precious pet on that dusty desert road.

Death Certificate

Some years ago, a lady who appeared to be in her late eighties or nineties lay on her deathbed at her home in Beverly Hills. Blood flowed from a catheter tube connected to her failed kidneys, as she lay in a coma. Her death certificate, bearing her doctor's signature, was on her dresser, ready for my mother, her nurse, to "Fill in the time of death when she expires."

We laid hands on the lady and, gently, asked God to raise her up so she could have one more chance to receive the LORD Jesus Christ as her Savior—before she slipped into eternity. We felt no tingling sensations or goosebumps, but within a minute, the woman's bodily functions started working. She opened her eyes, sat up in bed, said she was hungry and asked for a snack! Mom and I watched as pale-yellow fluid flowed down the clear plastic catheter tube, pushing the dark maroon-colored liquid all the way down the tube and into the bag below her bed.

The lady gave her heart to Jesus, and soon after, God gave her the ministry of intercession. She served Him faithfully for the rest of her days by agreeing in prayer for the needs of others as she watched live Christian television.

Bleeding Out

On April 22, 2014, an engaged couple (recovering drug addicts and God-softened felons) were hungry for God, in crisis, and needed His immediate help. For privacy's sake, let's call them *Tim* and *Tina*.

Tim's kidney function was down to 13 percent. He was not a transplant candidate. His doctor started surgery to insert a stent into *Tim's* chest for a dialysis connection.

Four hours into his operation, a nurse informed *Tina* that *Tim* was bleeding out on the operating table.

He was in surgery for over six hours when my daughter, Evelyn Rubidoux, called me. We asked God to stop the bleeding and raise *Tim* up. She asked me to call *Tina*, whom I had not met.

Tina and I remembered Jesus as we prayed together over the phone. And as we did, God's Word flooded our hearts, including the calming words of Psalm 23:4.

> Yea, though I walk through the valley of the shadow of death,
> I will fear no evil;
> For You *are* with me;
> Your rod and Your staff, they comfort me.　　　—Psalm 23:4 (NKJV)

We claimed God's peace and trusted in Jesus as His great promises kept coming. . .

> Weeping may endure for a night,
> But joy *comes* in the morning.
> 　　　　　　　—Psalm 30:5b (NKJV)

We clung to God's Word, not knowing if *Tim* would be having joy with *Tina* or joy with God in the morning.

> He sent His word and healed them,
> And delivered *them* from their destructions.　　—Psalm 107:20 (NKJV)

Heart Stopped

We were unaware that *Tim's* heart had stopped over an hour earlier. (The nurses in the operating room did not understand why *Tim's* doctor would not give up and why he kept trying for so long to bring Tim back to life.)

In Jesus's name, we spoke God's healing promises— with God's authority —not knowing we were talking to *Tim's* flat-lined body. We called him by name and boldly proclaimed, "*Tim!* Jesus said,"

> "It is the Spirit who gives life; the flesh profits nothing. The words that I speak to you are spirit, and *they* are life."　　—John 6:63 (NKJV)

We spoke *Tim's* name again and urged, "*Tim!* We send these words of life to you now and say, *live, Tim! Live! —In Jesus's name, LIVE!*" We broke the devil's hold over Tim from his life of crime. In Jesus's name, we ordered the devil to release him and claimed his freedom in Christ.

The urgency to pray lifted, and *Tina* and I were still chatting when a nurse said, "They're wheeling him out now."

At first, *Tina* did not know if they were wheeling *Tim* out to the morgue or back to his room.

We learned later that he had lost a lot of blood. His heart had been flat-lined over an hour and a half when the doctor finally sighed deeply, knowing he had to give up.

He stopped and looked up at the clock, ready to pronounce the time of death when—*Tim's heart started beating!*

The doctor told *Tina* what time it was when *Tim* came back to life. Her cell phone confirmed that Tim's life returned while we were praying. His heart started beating—when we spoke life to him in Jesus's Mighty Name!

Agreeing Prayer

Jesus worked with us and confirmed His Word (that we had claimed and spoken during our agreeing prayer)—with signs following—signs that crumbled death's stronghold on Tim and caused quite a stir in that hospital.

> Again I say unto you, that if two of you shall agree on earth as touching anything that they shall ask, it shall be done for them of my Father who is in heaven.   —Matthew 18:19 (ASV)

Healing of the Spiritually Dead

There are other dead that God wants us to help—the spiritually dead. We know that when we go in Jesus's name, He goes with us. When we speak or pray in His name, He does the work. Let's examine Matthew 18:19 a little more closely because it contains some conditions. If we meet God's requirements, we can have what we ask!

Interaction Between Earth and Heaven

Jesus began with the word "Again," which tells us that He must have already talked to them about something similar. What was it? Take a good look at verse eighteen.

> "Assuredly, I say to you, whatever you bind on earth will be bound in heaven, and whatever you loose on earth will be loosed in heaven."
> —Matthew 18:18 (NKJV)

So what does all of this mean? Well, obviously, Jesus was trying to help His followers to realize there is a connection between what people do on earth and what happens (or what comes from) heaven.

He Means You!

Jesus used the words *you, they,* and *them,* seven times in those two verses (Matthew 18:18–19). So what does that indicate?

He must mean that He expects you [us] to do something! That *something* is to *agree on earth.*

We must find someone who will focus on the Lord and not get all weird or go off into a religious frenzy. It is essential to be in harmony (one accord) when we ask God to help someone.

Be Specific

Notice that Jesus said, "concerning anything." He did not say, "concerning *everything.*" It is important to stay on the prayer topic because we cannot be in agreement if we are praying for different things.

For instance, if when we were praying for Tim, one of us was praying for Tim to pass away gently, and the other was asking God to raise him up, the outcome would probably have been different.

It is important to remember that Father God pays attention to what is happening where we are, and is ready and waiting to grant our petition—when we come into *agreement* with another person.

Then, to top it all off, Jesus went on to say,

> For where two or three are gathered together in my name, there am I in the midst of them.
> —Matthew 18:20 (ASV)

Guess who joins in with our agreeing prayers. It is none other than Jesus—Himself, our Great High Priest, and Great Intercessor!

Jesus, the Fourth Man in the fiery furnace (Daniel 3:24–25), is the Third Person in our midst, harmonizing with the intercession (prayers in two-part and three-part harmony) of *two or more* agreeing believers. Jesus, our Great High Priest, Mediator, and Advocate (attorney), lives forever to make intercession for His own.

> Therefore He is also able to save to the uttermost those who come to God through Him, since He always lives to make intercession for them.
> —Hebrews 7:25 (NKJV)

And that is not all. The Holy Spirit will add a new dynamic to your prayers as you walk boldly in your calling. He will equip and anoint you for whatever and wherever Jesus sends.

Comments:

_____
_____
_____
_____
_____
_____

***

---

[24] Webster's New Collegiate Dictionary; G. & C. Merriam Company, Springfield, MA, 1975, p. 364.

— By Mary A. Bruno, Ph.D.

> For our citizenship is in heaven, from which we also eagerly wait for the Savior, the Lord Jesus Christ,   —Philippians 3:20 (NKJV)

4
New Languages

The Reverend Doctor Rocco Bruno, my husband, was born and raised in Italy. His native language is Italian. I am a citizen of the United States of America, by birth. My native tongue is English. When Rocco received his US citizenship, he became a dual citizen of Italy and the USA. He is fluent in Italian, English, and Spanish, and was formerly fluent in French. He also understands Latin and Portuguese. When we were born again, we also became citizens of God's heavenly kingdom.

Most countries, lands, or kingdoms have a national language. How fitting that our Heavenly Father would give us the language of His kingdom, which helps us to communicate and to minister.

When Jesus fills us with the Holy Spirit, He also gives us His heavenly and earthly language(s) to enhance our communication.

Languages of Men and Angels

Which languages are spoken in Heaven? Paul's first letter to the Corinthians mentions the "tongues of men and angels" (1 Corinthians 13:1). God in Heaven listens to prayers in all languages and dialects of Planet Earth and answers in kind. Paul mentions the languages of angels. Notice the verse did *not* say *tongues* of men and tongue [singular] of angels. Might angels speak more than one language?

Baptism With the Holy Spirit

Speaking in "tongues" is a supernatural God-given ability beyond the natural ability to learn a native language or foreign language, through one's own power.

How does a believer get to speak in tongues?

According to Scripture, it happens when Jesus fills (baptizes/immerses/saturates) a believer and receiver with the Holy Spirit.

> And they were all filled with the Holy Spirit, and began to speak with other tongues, as the Spirit gave them utterance.   —Acts 2:4 (ASV)

Notice who did the speaking in Acts 2:4. *They*—not the Holy Spirit — spoke. *They* spoke (used their voices to utter the new syllables that became words) as the Holy Spirit gave them the ability to speak (to pronounce) the new sounds that

— By Mary A. Bruno, Ph.D.

became words, sentences, para-graphs, and conversation.

Equipped

Baptizing believers with the Holy Spirit is Jesus's way of outfitting them with the same Holy Spirit, and with the same power that He had to accomplish His ministry on earth. Jesus's very last words to His followers were:

> "But you shall receive power when the Holy Spirit has come upon you; and you shall be witnesses to Me in Jerusalem, and in all Judea and Samaria, and to the end of the earth."
> Now when He had spoken these things, while they watched, He was taken up, and a cloud received Him out of their sight.
> —Acts 1:8–9 (NKJV)

Virtue

As we may recall, that Greek word *dynamis* (du-na-mes) used for *power* in Acts 1:8, is the same word used for *virtue* in the account where Jesus felt *virtue* go out of Him when the woman with the issue of blood touched Him and received her healing (Mark 5:30).

Imagine that! This is what (Whom) we receive when Jesus fills us with His Holy Spirit—We get the same Holy Spirit Who equipped Jesus to fulfill His calling and miraculous ministry! No wonder the devil fights so hard to hide this great truth from believers. He knows if nominal Christians ever catch on to what they can have in Christ, the kingdom of darkness will crumble like a sandcastle at high tide.

Commissioned to Witness

The chosen generation knows being a witness for Christ is not only the natural result of a heart full of love and thanksgiving but is part of God's plan for every believer. God has no "Closet Christians." If we are truly His, we will claim and acknowledge our allegiance to Jesus the Christ before others. Thank God for the boldness that comes after being filled [baptized] with His Holy Spirit.

Because of His dynamic "power," we will dare to speak up in the most challenging circumstances. God's Spirit goes before us and prepares hearts to receive the gospel. While the person's heart is prepared and open—God counts on us to tell them about His love for them and of the joy and peace they can have in Christ.

As we are faithfully speaking God's message, His Spirit will be faithfully working in the other person(s)'s heart and convincing him or her or them the word is true, so he or she can believe, turn to Christ, and be saved, helped, healed, encouraged, and set free.

Wake up! Listen up! Speak up!

Isaiah may have understood the principle of God working with him when he penned these beautiful messianic words as follows,

> "The Lord GOD has given Me
> The tongue of the learned,
> That I should know how to speak
> A word in season to *him who is* weary
> He awakens Me morning by morning,
> He awakens My ear
> To hear as the learned.
> The Lord GOD has opened My ear;
> And I was not rebellious,
> Nor did I turn away."
>
> —Isaiah 50:4–5 (NKJV)

God will help us to hear and understand the message a person needs to hear. He will do this *daily* if we are willing and obedient to speak *all* that He entrusts to us.

Sent to Take the Gospel

The chosen generation is appointed and ordered (not merely recommended) to go with the gospel into the entire world.

> And He said to them, "Go into all the world and preach the gospel to every creature. He who believes and is baptized will be saved; but he who does not believe will be condemned."
> —Mark 16:15–16

God is urging us to spread the good news of His great Salvation and to preach wherever we go. Can He count on you to tell others about His gift of salvation?

__Yes. __No. ____Maybe.

> For, Whosoever shall call upon the name of the Lord shall be saved. How then shall they call on him in whom they have not believed? and how shall they believe in him whom they have not heard? and how shall they hear without a preacher? and how shall they preach, except they be sent? even as it is written, How beautiful are the feet of them that bring glad tidings of good things!   —Romans 10:13–15a ASV

As we are faithful to share God's Good News, Jesus will also be faithful to work with us and confirm His word with signs following, as we dare to demolish strongholds and magnify His name.

Loving one another with Jesus's love plays a big part in that.

In John's gospel, chapter fifteen, Jesus finished His message about *Abiding in the True Vine.* In the same breath, He went on to teach about abiding in His love; and gave this command—that was an order —not a suggestion:

> "This is My commandment, that you love one another as I have loved you. Greater love has no one than this, than to lay down one's life for his friends."   —John 15:12–13 (NKJV)

Do we dare to love one another with Christ's sacrificial love, even if doing so might make us feel uncomfortable at times?

If we love and care for someone, we will give them the information they need. We will do it NOW—so that he or she can believe on Christ, know His love, and escape an eternity of torment with a hateful smirking devil and his fallen angels. Love is the key. When a person knows we love and care about him or her, that one will be more likely to hear and receive what we have to say. The Bible warns:

> And as it is appointed for men to die once, but after this the judgment,
> —Hebrews 9:27 (NKJV)

For God's message to help us, we must believe and receive it while we are alive.

The Big Lie

Contrary to false teachings, there is no reincarnation or second chance after death. Scripture offers no such false hopes and does not mention purgatory. Some believe being baptized for their dead relatives will help them.

Some try to pray loved ones out of purgatory and ease their suffering for their sins. They need to see what God's Word says about trying to earn salvation by good works.

> For by grace you have been saved through faith, and that not of yourselves; *it is* the gift of God, not of works, lest anyone should boast.
> —Ephesians 2:8–9 (NKJV)

> "Let it be known to you all, and to all the people of Israel, that by the name of Jesus Christ of Nazareth, whom you crucified, whom God raised from the dead, by Him this man stands here before you whole. This is the 'stone which was rejected by you builders, which has become the chief cornerstone.' Nor is there salvation in any other, for there is no other name under heaven given among men by which we must be saved."   —Acts 4:10–12 (NKJV)

Jesus died (and rose again) to save sinners! If there were another way, God would not have needed to send His only begotten Son to become the only Sacrifice that can take away our sin.

Doctrines of demons offer false hope to the ignorant. Their poor victims will be horrified when they realize too late, they believed a lie and should have received the LORD Jesus Christ—the only Way to God. They will learn too late, there is no other name under heaven by which they could have been saved.

Comments:

_____

_____

_____

_____

_____

The chosen generation wears special garments.

* * *

— By Mary A. Bruno, Ph.D.

> *There were* twelve stones according to the names of the sons of Israel: according to their names, *engraved like* a signet, each one with its own name according to the twelve tribes.
> —Exodus 39:14 (NKJV)

5
Priestly Garments: Part 1

God's chosen generation and royal priesthood wear special garments. The Old Testament priests' apparel had special meaning. Knowing what the garments and colors represent will help one to understand the attire of New Testament priests who dare to pull down strongholds.

The Ephod

> And they shall make the ephod of gold, of blue, and purple, scarlet, and fine twined linen, the work of the skilful workman. It shall have two shoulder-pieces joined to the two ends thereof, that it may be joined together. And the skilfully woven band, which is upon it, wherewith to gird it on, shall be like the work thereof *and* of the same piece; of gold, of blue, and purple, and scarlet, and fine twined linen.
> —Exodus 28: 6–8 (ASV)

The ephod was an outer piece of clothing fashioned similarly to an apron or pinafore. It was made of linen and had fine threads of blue, purple, scarlet, and gold, woven into the fabric. [25]

Each color has symbolism: Blue draws our gaze beyond the blue sky to God in Heaven, where we look to Him for healing. Purple reminds us of Christ's royalty and our submission to His will. One day, King Jesus will return for all who have made Him their LORD.

Scarlet speaks of the scarlet thread of salvation, woven into God's plan down through the ages, and throughout Scripture. It represents Jesus's Holy Blood that purchased our salvation.

Gold symbolizes deity and reminds us that God wove Himself into His plan and is intricately involved in His dealings with man. He is as close to His kings and priests as the garments they wear. Perhaps, He wanted them to feel as if they were clothed with Him.

The Sash and Breastplate

Every priest had to wear a sash [belt] to hold his garments in place. Only when he was girded with his waistband, was he fully arrayed, prepared, and ready to serve.

> "You shall make the breastplate of judgment. Artistically woven according to the workmanship of . . .

— By Mary A. Bruno, Ph.D.

> "... the ephod you shall make it: of gold, blue, purple, and scarlet *thread,* and fine woven linen, you shall make it. It shall be doubled into a square: a span *shall be* its length, and a span *shall be* its width."
> —Exodus 28:15–16 (NKJV)

The breastplate was big enough to cover the priest's chest area [about 10–14 inches wide and 12–16 inches high]. Twelve precious stones, representing the twelve tribes of Israel, formed its covering. For further study, see Exodus 28:16-29, and 39:14-21.

The Urim and Thummim

The Urim ["light"] and Thummim ["perfection"] (God's perfect illumination) were both in the breastplate. They were involved in receiving divine guidance from God to His people. For further study, see Exodus 28:30, Numbers 27:21, and 1 Samuel 28:6.

The Robe, Turban, and Crown

The priest wore a sleeveless robe made of plain blue fabric under the ephod that resembled an apron. The robe was maybe a little longer than the ephod and had rows of embroidered pomegranates on the hem, interspaced with golden bells that tinkled as the priest moved.

The embroidered pomegranates (full of blood-red seeds) represented the life in God's Word. The sweet and precious seed of God's Word and the power of His blood make Jesus real to our hearts. It is fruitful, full of life, satisfies hungry souls, and helps us to trust in the cleansing power of His blood. (Exodus 28:31-35, 39:22-26)

Bells symbolized joy at the revelation and declaration of God's Word. They also assured the people their high priest was still alive while in the Holy place. Some priests were said to have gone in with unrepentant sin and died there in God's holy presence. They may have forgotten sin cannot abide in God's presence; therefore, we must be forgiven and cleansed before we die and must stand before Him.

The priest's hat was fashioned of white linen and was similar to a turban. It had a golden plate engraved with the words *Holiness to the Lord* fastened on the front. This represented the priest's true inner purity and mental purity, which God requires of all who serve Him.

Wearing the turban indicated the priest's commitment to live a holy life.

> "You shall skillfully weave the tunic of fine linen *thread,* you shall make the turban of fine linen, and you shall make the sash of woven work.
> "For Aaron's sons you shall make tunics, and you shall make sashes for them. And you shall make hats for. . ."

Choices & Stronghold

— By Mary A. Bruno, Ph.D.

> "... them, for glory and beauty. So you shall put them on Aaron your brother and on his sons with him. You shall anoint them, consecrate them, and sanctify them, that they may minister to Me as priests."
> —Exodus 28:39–41 (NKJV)

Let's dig a little deeper and examine the word meanings of: *anoint, consecrate, and sanctify,* which were part of becoming a priest to God in Exodus 28:41.

To *anoint,* (*mashach* Strong's H4886) means: to smear, anoint, spread a liquid. That liquid was oil, which is a type of the Holy Spirit.

To *consecrate,* (*male* (ma-la) Strong's H4390) means to: fill, full, fulfill, consecrate, overflow, and to be armed.

Note: After the Holy Spirit fell upon believers in Acts, chapter two, the New Testament kings and priests to God became Holy Spirit-filled, Holy Spirit-anointed, and Holy Spirit-armed, overcomers and champions in God's kingdom.

To *sanctify,* (*qadash*) ka-dash) Strong's H6942), means to: hallow, dedicate, holy, prepare, consecrate, appoint, and be separate.

The Anointing

Priests had to be clean to qualify for anointing with the special oil that poured over their heads and seeped down their garments. The anointing is a type of the Holy Spirit's infilling and coming upon, that equips for ministry. It happened when priests were consecrated and separated to God.

The New Testament attire is different but necessary for God's kings and priests who must enter into spiritual warfare and pull down strongholds. The chosen generation of New Testament priests must wear the complete armor of God, for many reasons, including the tearing down of strongholds.

The LORD has provided spiritual protection for the head and the entire body. Some have said there is protection for every part but the back, and if we turn away from the battle, we will be defenseless. I take exception to that line of thought because of Psalm 23:6, God's goodness and mercy will always back up His people.

Followed

Did you know you are being followed?

> Surely goodness and mercy shall follow me all the days of my life: and I will dwell in the house of the LORD for ever.
> —Psalm 23:6 (KJV)

God's goodness and mercy follow and protect believers. And if that were not enough, God has more for his fasting and prayer warriors. He even put it in print! Take a look. While looking, go ahead and draw a circle around every "you, your" and "yourself" in this passage.

> "*Is* this not the fast that I have chosen:
> To loose the bonds of wickedness,
> To undo the heavy burdens,
> To let the oppressed go free,
> And that you break every yoke?"
> *Is it* not to share your bread with the hungry,
> And that you bring to your house the poor who are cast out;
> When you see the naked, that you cover him,
> And not hide yourself from your own flesh?
> Then your light shall break forth like the morning,
> Your healing shall spring forth speedily,
> And your righteousness shall go before you;
> The glory of the LORD shall be your *rear guard*.
> Then you shall call, and the LORD will answer;
> You shall cry, and He will say, 'Here I *am*.'
> "If you take away the yoke from your midst,
> The pointing of the finger,
> and speaking wickedness,"
> —Isaiah 58:6–9 (NKJV) Emphasis added

The words *rear guard*, in the above passage, imply "A military detachment detailed to bring up and protect the rear part of a main body or force." God's glory (the magnificent manifestation of His Almighty Presence) shall guard and protect the backside of His troops (belie-vers). When the LORD of Hosts takes up the back slack, we are fully covered, and none can defeat us!

And while exploring the passage, let's not overlook that beautiful word *healing* in verse 8. It is from the Hebrew word *aruwkah (Strong's H724)*, which implies: *restoring to soundness, wholeness, healing,* and *restoration,* with the idea of a long bandage binding up a wound (or winding like a turban on one's head) so that it can heal.

This brings to mind Jesus's healing provision for the whole person—including mental disorders, such as Bipolar, Schizophrenia, Post-Traumatic Stress Disorder (PTSD), Dementia, and others.

This word (healing) has likewise translated in Scripture as: *health, perfected,* and *made up.* Our healing will spring forth *speedily* when we fast and pray for others. [26]

> Confess *your* trespasses to one another, and pray for one another, that **you** may be healed. The effective, fervent prayer of a righteous man avails much.
> —James 5:16 (NKJV) Emphasis added

This is another promise of healing that happens when we pray for each other. Jesus unexpectedly confirmed this. In January 2014, I tripped and tore a tendon in my right ankle that kept getting worse. After 18 months of pain (most of which were on crutches), and three canceled surgeries, a specialist said the tendon had *deteriorated* [was rotten.] —Not what we had hoped to hear.

In 2015 Rocco and I taught an IMI Bible College & Seminary degree program at a church in Vista, California. For month-after-month, I hobbled in on crutches and sat to teach. Standing would have been my preference because teaching God's Word is very exciting and makes one want to move around.

Gabriel (made-up name), was an excellent student with a godly wife (also a student of IMIBCS), whom we shall call Angela (not her real name). *Gabe*, one of God's extra special people, loved Jesus and loved to serve. Gabe's doctor found a lump on his neck in late June and sent him for immediate tests. Gabriel's condition rapidly declined, and he could not attend class.

In mid-August, while still on crutches and hurting from the deteriorated tendon, God led me to fast and pray for *Gabriel*. On day two of the fast, the crutches became more of a hindrance than a help, so I laid them aside, switched to a cane, and kept fasting and praying for Gabe. On day four of the fast, my cane kept getting in the way. I set it aside and kept praying for *Gabriel's healing*.

At 12:20 p.m. on day Day Four — Gabriel was with Jesus.

God took Gabriel home and healed my tendon on the same day.

His ways are a mystery that we may understand when we get to Heaven. I had hoped Gabriel would go on to help us with the Bible College, but God loved him too and wanted Gabriel closer to Him.

That happened over three years ago (at the time of this writing). My ankle and tendon are still pain-free.

Is the Lord bringing someone to your mind right now and giving you the desire to pray for his or her healing or other need? Father God may have that person's answer to prayer all ready to go, and is just waiting for someone to pray for his or her need, so that He can release the answer.

Go ahead! Pray for him or her! The worst that could happen is, Father God might get extra blessed from hearing you pray, but that's a good thing and He can handle it.

* * *

Comments:

_____

_____

---

[25] L. Thomas Holdcroft, The Pentateuch, pp. 78, 79.

[26] "H724 - 'aruwkah - Strong's Hebrew Lexicon (KJV)." Blue Letter Bible. Accessed 8 Dec, 2018. https://www.blueletterbible.org//lang/Lexicon/Lexicon.cfm?Strongs=H724&t=KJV

> Put on the whole armor of God, that you may be able to stand against the wiles of the devil. —Ephesians 6:11 (NKJV)

6

Priestly Garments: Part 2

Unlike the priests of old, New Testament priests to God do not design their priestly attire from materials of this world. Their covering is spiritual. God's armor is defined as follows.

New Testament Garments and the Armor of God

> Put on the whole armor of God, that you may be able to stand against the wiles of the devil. For we do not wrestle against flesh and blood, but against principalities, against powers, against the rulers of the darkness of this age, against spiritual *hosts* of wickedness in the heavenly *places.* Therefore take up the whole armor of God, that you may be able to withstand in the evil day, and having done all, to stand.
> —Ephesians 6:11–13 (NKJV)

> Stand therefore, having girded your waist with truth, having put on the breastplate of righteousness, and having shod your feet with the preparation of the gospel of peace; above all, taking the shield of faith with which you will be able to quench all the fiery darts of the wicked one. And take the helmet of salvation, and the sword of the Spirit, which is the word of God; praying always with all prayer and supplication in the Spirit, being watchful to this end with all perseverance and supplication for all the saints—
> —Ephesians 6:14–18 (NKJV)

New Testament gladiators had to wrestle in hand-to-hand combat unto death. Believers also wrestle—with sin and evil—knowing, if we do not overcome the sin and evil—it will destroy us.

Mandatory Attire

Wearing God's armor is not optional. It is a *command.* New Testament kings and priests to God, minister to the LORD, Himself, with praise, worship, thanksgiving, offerings of gifts, and intercession. We must also wear God's protective armor; stay filled with, and be led by His Holy Spirit, as we engage in active resistance and warfare against the devil and his territorial rulers.

Stand for God

There are many falls in a wrestling match, but only one victory. The

— By Mary A. Bruno, Ph.D.

enemy is always looking for an unprotected place where the believer is weak or most vulnerable. If you get knocked down and happen to lose a piece of your armor during the battle, ask God to replace it; then, get up, get back in the fight, and seize your victory!

To *stand* means to be *alert* and *on guard* as a soldier standing watch. Do not let the tempter in, or let anything sneak by when taking a stand for God.

How Wiles Work

The wearing of God's armor enables believers to take a firm stand against the wiles of the devil.

What, exactly, is a *wile*?

It comes from a word meaning to *lie in wait to deceive,* and is associated with the mentality, methods, and strategies involved in setting traps to trick or deceive someone.

Women are, said to use their wiles to catch their men. They primp, preen, and polish; nip, snip, and curl, and then pluck, press, perfume, and powder, until all looks great on the outside. She speaks in soft tones and listens with interest to every word the targeted man utters. She expresses support and enthusiasm for his visions, goals, and dreams and convinces him she believes he is the greatest man on earth and able to achieve any feat. She presents herself with a *Come-hither* look that promises to be the answer to all of his hopes and prayers for a mate.

If God blesses the union, and her wiles work, the woman ends up with a ring on her finger. If the wiles work, but God does not bless their union, the man could end up with a thorn in his side and a ring in his nose!

God's armor will protect the believer's mind, with wisdom, strength, and self-control, and keep him or her from being hooked or trapped by ungodly tactics, tricks, and devices.

Principalities

Against whom do we wrestle? We grapple against principalities—evil territorial rulers. One may wonder why certain countries, cities, etc., seem to be plagued with a tendency toward a certain kind of sin or vice.

Over Cities and Nations

Take, for instance, the city of Las Vegas, known as *Sin City.* What comes to mind? Gambling, and of course, greed and sexual vice. That city of bright lights may be under the dark influence of demonic spirits of gaming (chance), greed, and lust.

Evil principalities can oppress people of other beautiful cities, islands, nations, and dismal slums. In many countries, principalities hold the inhabitants captive through false religions and idolatry.

Choices & Strongholds

— By Mary A. Bruno, Ph.D.

We Wrestle

The Bible says we wrestle against *rulers of darkness*—ungodly administrations working in the world around us, "against spiritual wickedness in high places." Evil rulers and demonic powers know they must obey God's servants' commands. They know when Christians resist them; they must fold up camp, forfeit positions, and flee.

New Testament priests and overcomers do not get to pick and choose their uniforms. They must wear the whole armor of God.

Truth Ties it Together

Weightlifters use heavy belts to protect their vital organs when they exert themselves to maximum endurance. God's wide band of truth preserves believers who are wise and obedient enough to clothe themselves with the truth. When one knows God's Word and is committed to abide by it, God's truth will protect the loins of his or her body, soul, and spirit. Kings and priests to God must have no part in lying—not even one *polite* lie or *little white* lie! There is no such thing as a *little white lie*. All lies are evil.

"But the cowardly, unbelieving, abominable, murderers, sexually immoral, sorcerers, idolaters, and all liars shall have their part in the lake which burns with fire and brimstone, which is the second death."
—Revelation 21:8 (NKJV)

Breastplate of Righteousness

God gives protection for the upper body. The breastplate shields the front and back, offering coverage from the neck to the hips. It covers one's strength and emotions [often enemy targets] and problems associated with them. Christ's righteousness is credited to every believer and becomes his or her breastplate. Few may recognize this protective power, but God does.

Gospel Shoes

God's soldiers must protect their feet with the preparation of the Gospel of peace. In the New Testament times, armies frequently set landmine traps by burying sticks and daggers where invading troops would march. The preparation of the gospel of peace will take believers safely to wherever God sends them. When on a mission for God—not on a vacation to Sodom and Gomorrah—they will march triumphantly straight through enemy territory. The gospel shoes will take them on short missions and long journeys.

The chosen generation must stay ready to take God's message of peace without bitterness or discord.

When warring with the devil, we are, most likely, at peace with God. If we are playing around and at peace with the devil, we are usually at war with God. As the saying goes,

Choices & Strongholds

— By Mary A. Bruno, Ph.D.

"Pick your battles carefully. Choose the ones that you can win."

The gospel shoes keep us running with God's burning love that melts cold hearts. The gospel is good news! Believers must bring a message of hope and joy, and not just doom and gloom. Gospel shoes are the right size for every believer. They will continue to fit as we grow.

Shield of Faith vs. Fiery Darts

God gives all in His Army the shield of faith, which quenches the fiery darts of the wicked one. That shield is big enough to protect the entire person. Ancient shields were made of boards, linen, nails, and leather. The wood reminds us of the Cross, the linen of Christ's righteousness; the nails call to mind the spikes that pierced Jesus's hands and feet. Leather reminds us of sacrifice [something had to die to yield the leather]. Christ's divine sacrifice—with blood—was given for our salvation and protection.

That shield of faith will stop all of the enemy's flaming darts of pride; envy; jealousy; revenge; hatred; evil passions, cravings, unbelief, etcetera. The shield of faith reminds soldiers we are out to win the whole war—not just a few battles. Troops marching in rank and order may encounter a sudden attack. If they continue to stand side-by-side, and shield-to-shield, nothing can penetrate their ranks that are like a mighty mobile wall of faith/shields.

More than Intellectual Acknowledgement

The shield of faith is more than mere intellectual agreement with the truth. It means to *embrace* the gospel with one's whole heart. Shield-faith is not based on feelings but holds firmly to God's written Word and faithfulness. Shield-faith is vital for victory.

It cultivates a victorious relationship with Jesus. As we consult with Him about decisions, etc., we learn to recognize His voice and His Presence and trust Him more.

Helmet of Salvation

The chosen generation wears the helmet of salvation, which is a gift from Jesus, the Captain of our salvation. It protects the mind from fear and deception, and improves divine communication. It protects the wearer from confusion or other mental attacks, and helps God's soldiers to receive His strategies.

A capable overcomer will dare to thrust a sharp sword (sharp Scripture) that inflicts massive damage to enemy strongholds.

Comments:

———————————————————
———————————————————
———————————————————

* * *

> For the weapons of our war-
> fare *are* not carnal but mighty
> in God for pulling down strong-
> holds, casting down arguments
> and every high thing that exalts
> itself against the knowledge of
> God, bringing every thought into
> captivity to the obedience of
> Christ,   —2 Corinthians 10:4–5 (NKJV)

7

Authority and Weapons: Part 1

We must be willing to take hold of the sword of the Spirit (which the Spirit wields)—the written Word of God—and dare to use it in battles against evil. Human opinions and traditions are as worthless as squirt guns during spiritual warfare. Relying on traditions, rituals, or anything except God's Word will be very disappointing when dealing with strongholds. But those who do things God's way will have good results that will set people free to live for the LORD.

Sharp Sword

God's Word is sharp enough to cut through the evil one's stinging lies and accusations. The Holy Spirit knows how to give a *word in season* for those who trust in Him.

The *Sword of Damascus* was made by those who resided in Damascus. The *Sword of the Spirit* (a spiritual sword) was created by God's Spirit when He inspired and moved upon holy men of old. Down through the ages, He stirred His servants to write inspired *verbal plenary* (Every word is inspired by God.) messages from God to His people. That Holy Writ (The Bible) wells up within believers as a mighty weapon of war. The sword's Maker (God) teaches His troops how to wield their swords and win battles.

> Every scripture inspired of
> God *is* also profitable for teaching,
> for reproof, for correction,
> for instruction which is in
> righteousness: that the man of God
> may be complete, furnished
> completely unto every good work
>   —2 Timothy 3:16–17 (ASV)

How does one obtain the sword of the Spirit? This comes by studying the Bible, by comparing spiritual with spiritual, by praying for under-standing and illumination, by Scrip-ture memorization, and by hearing anointed teaching and preaching.

Armor and Prayer

Pray and keep on praying, with all kinds of prayer. Pray in your heav-enly language. (If you have not

— By Mary A. Bruno, Ph.D.

received that ability yet—ask Jesus to baptize you with the Holy Spirit, and then receive His gift.) After receiving this gift you will be able to switch back and forth between your native language, and tongues.

It is amazing how creative and insightful prayers in one's native tongue become after praying for a while in *tongues*. Praying in the spirit includes inspired prayers with the understanding as well as in the spirit. Both are needful. Believers must live in an attitude of open communication with God.

> Then Peter said to them, "Repent, and let every one of you be baptized in the name of Jesus Christ for the remission of sins; and you shall receive the gift of the Holy Spirit. For the promise is to you and to your children, and to all who are afar off, as many as the Lord our God will call." —Acts 2:38–39 (NKJV)

Phrase Check

Just as soldiers must clean their weapons, it is a good idea to have a *phrase check* from time to time, to clean up any repeat phrases that have become conversational *crutches or verbal fluff* in our prayer life. Doing so may help to keep us from lapsing into a stale routine that could become boring and vain repetition. It is not uncommon for this to crop up in one's prayer life.

Moreover, people may hear a prominent preacher on TV praying up a storm. The next thing you know, many across the country are parroting the preacher's favorite prayer phrases. God has given enough words to go around for all of us. Why should we imitate someone else's prayer when it is more fun to come up with our own? God appreciates fresh and thoughtful conversation.

The basic principles of prayer (communication with God) remain the same, but fresh wording is refreshing.

Stay on Watch

The chosen generation must watch. To *watch* has to do with more than a casual glance, or lingering gaze [which is how David got into trouble with Bathsheba in Second Samuel 11:1–5]. It means to be *alert* and *at attention* (not idle), and ready to take action. Believers should never let down their guard or fall into a dull state of slumber, but must stay alert with earnest prayer. We must continually serve the LORD with all of our mind, soul, and strength.

Let's use our time wisely and serve God to the utmost of our ability, according to His power and presence at work within us. Let's stay ready like the five wise virgins in the parable (story with a lesson) that Jesus taught.

Choices & Strongholds — By Mary A. Bruno, Ph.D.

> "Then the kingdom of heaven shall be likened to ten virgins who took their lamps and went out to meet the bridegroom. Now five of them were wise, and five *were* foolish. Those who *were* foolish took their lamps and took no oil with them, but the wise took oil in their vessels with their lamps. But while the bridegroom was delayed, they all slumbered and slept.
>
> "And at midnight a cry was *heard:* 'Behold, the bridegroom is coming; go out to meet him!' Then all those virgins arose and trimmed their lamps. And the foolish said to the wise, 'Give us *some* of your oil, for our lamps are going out.' But the wise answered, saying, '*No,* lest there should not be enough for us and you; but go rather to those who sell, and buy for yourselves.' And while they went to buy, the bridegroom came, and those who were ready went in with him to the wedding; and the door was shut.
>
> "Afterward the other virgins came also, saying, 'Lord, Lord, open to us!' But he answered and said, 'Assuredly, I say to you, I do not know you.'
>
> "Watch therefore, for you know neither the day nor the hour in which the Son of Man is coming."
> —Matthew 25:1–13 (NKJV)

Slumber and neglect were the downfalls of the unwise who failed to plan and got left out. The wise ones were prepared with oil (a symbol of the Holy Spirit) in anticipation of the bridegroom's coming and had a great outcome.

While watching and praying, God may reveal ungodly things that have been cropping up like weeds in one's life. He usually brings them to light when it is time for them to go—because He wants to make room to replace them with something much better, more desirable, and useful.

Mulberry Tree

The chosen generation is authorized to uproot.

> And the apostles said to the Lord, "Increase our faith."
> So the Lord said, "If you have faith as a mustard seed, you can say to this mulberry tree, 'Be pulled up by the roots and be planted in the sea,' and it would obey you."
> —Luke 17:5–6 (NKJV)

I got to wondering why anyone would want to cast a tree into the sea. A mulberry (sycamine) tree produces fruit that looks similar to very long, skinny boysenberries. The fruit can be either white or deep bluish-red.

Now suppose that tree was contaminated and produced fruit that could make one sick. Think about your children or yourself eating from the diseased tree and getting stained and ill (similar to sin's dark stain on one's soul). This might

Choices & Strongholds

— By Mary A. Bruno, Ph.D.

motivate a parent to order the diseased fruit tree to pluck up and go to where it cannot grow. Some people are like diseased mulberry trees spreading their influence to defile anyone willing to partake of their corruption. When they affect you, your church, or your loved ones, it is time to exercise your authority to uproot their influence.

Family Tree

There is another kind of tree, with which all of us must reckon—the family tree. God may have brought to your attention a repeated pattern of ungodly behavior (alcoholism, drug addiction, perversion, crime, idolatry, illegitimacy, witchcraft, incest, etc.) that has passed down from generation to generation in your family. If so, you may be dealing with a principality at work in your bloodline.

When you discern a spirit—deal with it! Confront it and, as Jesus authorized, *command* it to be plucked up by the root and cast into the sea, never again to oppress anyone in your bloodline. Then—Lo and Behold!—Jesus said, "And it will obey you."

Jesus did not say to ask Him to do it. This is why He delegated the authority to *you*. He wants you to grow up, be brave, be bold, exercise your rights in Christ, and order the ungodly spirit to leave.

Unfruitful Obstacles

The disciples were amazed at how little time it took for the fig tree to wither away after Jesus cursed it. It happened overnight. Imagine their surprise when Jesus said:

> "Assuredly, I say to you, if you have faith and do not doubt, you will not only do what was done to the fig tree, but also if you say to this mountain, 'Be removed and be cast into the sea,' it will be done. And whatever things you ask in prayer, believing, you will receive."
> —Matthew 21:21b–22 (NKJV)

Why might Jesus have used the word *you* six times in those two sentences? A diligent student of the Word might think Jesus wants us to focus on the word, *you*.

Notice what Jesus said His followers could do. He said (if they (you) have faith) they (you) would get to do what He did to the fig tree. What did Jesus do to that tree?

He spoke up and then confronted and cursed the unfruitful thing. And when He did, it withered away (overnight.)

Jesus authorized us to do the same thing. Do you need to deal with any fruitless areas in your life or ministry that take up space, soak up supplies, and produce nothing of value? The change can happen within hours or overnight if you dare to do things God's way and confront the encroacher. Remember, this was a *thing*—not a person—that Jesus cursed.

Authority to Move Mountains

How does one go about exercising his or her biblical authority to cast mountains into the sea?

As we read in Matthew 21:21, Jesus gave His followers (including us) authority to cast mountains into the sea. Mountains (barriers of dirt, uncleanness, or obstacles) can be humanly impossible to move.

Jesus said we could order the mountains (in life and ministry) to be removed and cast into the sea.

How does one do that?

1. Identify the mountain.

2. Confront the specific mountain (problem).

3. Command the mountain (obstacle) to be removed.

Go ahead and do it right now. Speak an authoritative word (command) to the mountain that needs to go. This is not a time to pray and ask God to do something.

As His delegate, He expects *you* to be brave and use your God-given authority.

4. The mountain must obey you when you do what God said you could do.

If your faith is not ready for a full-size mountain or tree, then build it up by starting with a *spiritual* *molehill* or *shrub* and work your way up to a full-size mountain or tree!

5. Satan likes to make mountains out of our molehills. But, Jesus authorized you to make molehills out of his mountains!

Years ago, when I had more faith than money, some tree roots caused nasty black sewer water to back up overnight (four inches deep!) into our white bathtub at Temple City, California. I stretched out my hand over the revolting water, commanded those roots to be plucked up and cast into the sea, and then drove to my job at World Vision International in Monrovia. The black water was gone when I got home. As I recall, we had no more problems with it while we owned that house.

As part of the chosen generation and royal priesthood, we must use our authority over spiritual wickedness and pull down strongholds wherever we find them.

Comments

_____

_____

_____

_____

_____

_____

* * *

> "See, I have this day set you over the nations and over the kingdoms,
> To root out and to pull down,
> To destroy and to throw down,
> To build and to plant."
> —Jeremiah 1:10 (NKJV)

8
Authority and Weapons: Part 2

In Jeremiah 1:10, God gave His servant, Jeremiah, authority over nations and kingdoms, including bases of operations in the natural and spiritual realms. As we know,

> Every scripture inspired of God *is* also profitable for teaching, for reproof, for correction, for instruction which is in righteousness: — 2 Timothy 3:16 (ASV)

Nations and Kingdoms

We are authorized to root out that which produces corrupt fruit. We get to root out the enemy's central intelligence system (his strong-holds). When we dare to deal with the root, the fruit will stop.

We have the authority to pull down that which God has not established in families, ministries, and nations. Daniel pulled down a principality through fasting and prayer. It took three weeks and an angel—but he got it done.

We have authority to overthrow what the enemy has established for himself in our bloodline, and to throw down principalities behind every evil work.

We are authorized to build and plant on the foundation of God's written Word and the LORD Jesus Christ. We get to sow God's Holy Word and reap a holy harvest of souls filled with the sweet fruit of His Holy Spirit.

Devils and Diseases

God gave believers authority over all devils and diseases.

> And he called the twelve together, and gave them power and authority over all demons, and to cure diseases. And he sent them forth to preach the kingdom of God, and to heal the sick. —Luke 9:1–2 (ASV)

Jesus not only, gave His disciples power and authority over all demons, but to cure diseases (plural), and if that were not enough, He sent them to preach the kingdom of God and to heal the sick.

But, some may say, "That was then. This is now. Things are

different today." Yes, times do change. Yet, the Bible tells us,

> Jesus Christ *is* the same yesterday, today, and forever.
> —Hebrews 13:8 (NKJV)

Jesus Christ is the same today as he was before His Crucifixion and after His Resurrection. He continues to teach, authorize, and empower His students. A student who rightly applies his lessons will surely please his or her teacher.

Jesus must smile when we follow His instructions.

> And he rose up from the synagogue, and entered into the house of Simon. And Simon's wife's mother was holden with a great fever; and they besought him for her. And he stood over her, and rebuked the fever; and it left her: and immediately she rose up and ministered unto them.
> —Luke 4:38–39a (ASV)

Rebuke

Jesus demonstrated how to exercise His power and authority over sickness and disease. In the case of Peter's mother-in-law, Jesus did not lay His hands on her. He did not pray for her. Jesus did not command her to get up. He stood over her and *rebuked the fever*. And when he dared to confront the fever, *it left immediately*, and she got up and got back to work at what she did well. She served the Lord and others.

He touched some, and others touched Him, yet all were healed. Each incident was different; Jesus never fell into a stale routine.

Dare to be bold and courageous as you take new steps of faith and obedience. Dare to follow the LORD's example and leading. When we dare to rebuke a fever or disease in Jesus's name, He will back us up, and it will go.

The Weapons

The chosen generation and royal priesthood use spiritual weapons:

> For the weapons of our warfare *are* not carnal but mighty in God for pulling down strongholds, casting down arguments and every high thing that exalts itself against the knowledge of God, bringing every thought into captivity to the obedience of Christ,
> —2 Corinthians 10:4–5 (NKJV)

The Weapon of God's Word

God's written Word is our primary weapon in spiritual warfare. Great things happen when we apply His Word at the right time, in the right place, in the right spirit, for the right reasons, which is a good reason to commit it to memory.

Choices & Strongholds

— By Mary A. Bruno, Ph.D.

Authority to Bind

We have it in writing! See it for yourself. Jesus said to believers,

> "Assuredly, I say to you, whatever you bind on earth will be bound in heaven, and whatever you loose on earth will be loosed in heaven."
> —Matthew 18:18 (NKJV)

Have you bound or loosed anything lately?

God gave us this authority because He knew we would need it. When we speak according to His Word, He will enforce it. He does so because He knows that what we say and *whatever* we bind will be according to His will (What Jesus would bind if He were standing in our shoes) and that we are acting as His commissioned agents.

Speaking of agents, when selling a car and buying another, our insurance agent assured by phone, the coverage was transferred from the old car to the new one. We had nothing in writing at that moment but knew the new car was covered because our insurance company's agent had issued a verbal *binder* while we were speaking, which they were required to uphold.

> And it shall come to pass that, before they call, I will answer; and while they are yet speaking, I will hear.
> —Isaiah 65:24 (ASV)

We have a similar binding privilege for *whatever* we bind in Jesus's name. We even have it in writing!

Power of Attorney

Rocco and I traveled to Italy while our house was for sale. Naturally, we wanted to do all we could to help it sell quickly. So, we gave my mother power of attorney for that particular transaction. We authorized her to accept a reasonable offer on the house and to open an escrow account in our name. Whatever she signed for that house was legally binding on us. We had to honor her word and all the decisions that she made while acting as our agent.

When someone presented a fair offer, Mother accepted it and signed the contract. The escrow closed two weeks after we returned to the States, and we were able to buy a better house.

Authority to Restrain

That power of attorney was similar to the privilege God gave to His children. When we act in His name and according to His will, our words are legally binding on Him. When we find the enemy at work, we can bind him. When we do so, God promised that before we call and, while we are still speaking—He will hear and answer.

This is similar to a legal restraining order but not like the kind we have in California where someone with a restraining order against them can still walk up and shoot a harassed person.

We get to issue binding orders on evil entities and order them to leave and not return. When we give commands in Jesus's name (acting as His agents), God enforces them and puts all the power of Heaven behind our words! The evil spirit knows it must stop what it was doing and leave.

The Weapon of Jesus's Blood

When believers dare to use Jesus's blood and His Word as weapons, who can stand against them?

> And they overcame him because of the blood of the Lamb, and because of the word of their testimony; and they loved not their life even unto death. —Revelation 12:11 (ASV)

Jesus's shed blood defeated Satan. Declaring the power of His precious blood is an explosive weapon for every believer. If you notice any of God's children being oppressed by the devil or an unclean spirit, merely remind the entity that this person is God's child, purchased with Jesus's Holy Blood. Tell the evil spirit it has no authority to hold him or her. Tell it to let go and leave. As mentioned previously, this is what Tina and I did when Tim was flat-lined on the operating table.

The Weapon of Jesus's Name

Jesus's name is an excellent weapon for every believer. We must agree with the mind of Christ and remember Jesus works with us.

> Let this mind be in you which was also in Christ Jesus, who, being in the form of God, did not consider it robbery to be equal with God, but made Himself of no reputation, taking the form of a bondservant, *and* coming in the likeness of men. And being found in appearance as a man, He humbled Himself and became obedient to *the point of* death, even the death of the cross. Therefore God also has highly exalted Him and given Him the name which is above every name, that at the name of Jesus every knee should bow, of those in heaven, and of those on earth, and of those under the earth, and *that* every tongue should confess that Jesus Christ *is* Lord, to the glory of God the Father. —Philippians 2:5–11 (NKJV)

Coming Attractions

One day, Hitler, Buddha, Satan, Confucius, witches, warlocks, atheists, etc., will bow before the LORD Jesus Christ, and confess Jesus Christ is LORD. No other name has the power of Jesus's name.

Let's exercise our authority over the voice-trained enemy.

Comments:

_____

* * *

> "Assuredly, I say to you,
> whatever you bind on earth will
> be bound in heaven, and
> whatever you loose on earth will
> be loosed in heaven."
> —Matthew 18:18 (NKJV)

9
Voice-trained Enemy

Some time ago, while speaking for an Aglow meeting in Stockton, California, I met a police officer who was assigned to a K-9 division of the police department. He had a big scary-looking, voice-trained dog that was a K-9 officer. At times, the animal acted ferociously and scared all close to him. But when his trainer spoke an order, the dog/K-9 officer sat down and was as sweet as a pup.

The dog had undergone obedience training and voice training. When he learned to obey his trainer's voice commands, he earned his credentials and an assignment to work with that particular police officer.

He Obeys Your Voice Command

In a way, Jesus has done that with the devil. The LORD has obedience-trained and voice-trained the devil and his cohorts to obey a believer's voice command that is issued in Jesus's name. (Trying this in *your* name may bring unwanted results.)

All we need to do is exercise our God-given authority and do what He authorized us to do—give a command. The obedience-trained enemy knows he must settle down, back off, shut his mouth, and obey your order. Doing so will bring freedom and peace. And if you choose not to exercise your privilege, the enemy may laugh at you, stir things up, and make a big mess.

> Not that we are sufficient of
> ourselves, to account anything as
> from ourselves; but our sufficiency is
> from God;   —2 Corinthians 3:5 (ASV)

The Finger of God

God's Holy Spirit is the believer's "Secret Weapon." Jesus taught the following about His power:

> But if I cast out demons with the finger
> of God, surely the kingdom of God has
> come upon you. When a strong man,
> fully armed, guards his own palace, his
> goods are in peace. But when a
> stronger than he comes upon him and
> overcomes him, he takes from him all
> his armor in which he trusted, and
> divides his spoils. —Luke 11:20–22 (NKJV)

By the power of God's Holy Spirit—Who lives within us!—we can tear down enemy strongholds wherever

— By Mary A. Bruno, Ph.D.

we find them and liberate the captives, including people, positions, and things.

Strip-Search

The Holy Spirit's power and anointing will strip away all of an evil entity's (strongman's) protective armor (Luke 11:20–22), and leave him as bare and exposed as a defeated soldier stripped down to his underwear. When this happens, the oppressing spirit will lose faith in his devices and tricks, realize he lost, surrender what he stole, and depart in defeat.

Furthermore, the thief must pay back twice what he stole (pay more than full restitution), and at times he must restore sevenfold.

> "If a man delivers to his neighbor money or articles to keep, and it is stolen out of the man's house, if the thief is found, he shall pay double."
> —Exodus 22:7 (NKJV)

> Men do not despise a thief, if he steal
> To satisfy himself when he is hungry:
> But if he be found, he shall restore sevenfold;
> He shall give all the substance of his house.　　—Proverbs 6:30–31 (ASV)

Disarmed

The enemy's weapons and armor include lies; unrighteousness; unrest; spiritual blindness; unbelief; spiritual death; false doctrines; prayerlessness, and so on.

When a Spirit-filled believer dares to step in and take authority over an unclean spirit and his devices, the evil being must depart from that victim or circumstance.

Submission and Resistance

Submission and resistance are weapons that work.

> But He gives more grace. Therefore He says:
> "God resists the proud,
> But gives grace to the humble."
> Therefore submit to God. Resist the devil and he will flee from you.
> —James 4:6–7 (NKJV)

In every trial or test, we must make choices. Will we yield to the evil one, or our fleshly cravings, and oppose God? Or, will we surrender to God, control our sensual desires, and resist the evil one?

The book of James commands us to, "Submit yourselves therefore to God." Notice the promise with the command: "Resist"—not play around with—"the devil and he will flee from you." (James 4:7).

We must discipline (train) ourselves to promptly surrender to God. After a while, the evil one will realize we will not give up or give in at the drop of a hint or wile.

When he realizes we have taken a firm stand for God, and against him, he will avoid us, make a hasty retreat from our presence, and search out more ignorant prey. (Being shunned by the devil is not a bad thing.)

God's chosen generation has a new position of authority and supernatural power from God.

Holy Spirit's Power

As stated in the preceding chapter, Jesus gave power to His followers (to His royal priesthood.)

> And he called the twelve together, and gave them power and authority over all demons, and to cure diseases. And he sent them forth to preach the kingdom of God, and to heal the sick.   —Luke 9:1–2 (ASV)

Jesus empowered His disciples (which includes us) and expects them to exercise His power over all devils; to cure diseases; to preach the kingdom of God (When was the last time you heard a sermon about God's Kingdom?), and to heal those who are sick.

God gave us His power—not for us to display on the mantle, but for us to use. Let's dare use it! Jesus gave His disciples, including us, power over how many devils?

Jesus gave us power over *all* shapes, sizes, and ranks of devils!

Forward March

As if that were not enough, Jesus added more.

> Then the seventy returned with joy, saying, "Lord, even the demons are subject to us in Your name."
>
> And He said to them, "I saw Satan fall like lightning from heaven.
>
> Behold, I give you the authority to trample on serpents and scorpions, and over all the power of the enemy, and nothing shall by any means hurt you. Nevertheless do not rejoice in this, that the spirits are subject to you, but rather rejoice because your names are written in heaven."   —Luke 10:17–20 (NKJV)

Jesus never intended for us to get wild-eyed and start playing with poisonous snakes. This passage is about dealing with the powers of evil. When we encounter them, they cannot harm us.

To tread on serpents and scorpions is a type of using our God-given power and authority over all of the enemy's devices. This power is not a license to show off with a slithering serpentine sideshow.

Stay Christ-Centered

Believers must stay Christ-centered—and not focus on the devil. It is essential to confront the enemy and command him to leave while keeping our mind stayed on Christ. Christians should not give free publicity to God's enemy, especially when ministering in public.

No free Advertising!

There is often no need to address the devil publicly in prayer and bind him every time before bringing a message from God's Word. When we feel the need to restrict demonic influence, we usually can do it privately—before stepping to the microphone. By keeping our hearts stayed on Jesus and avoiding such distractions, the audience's attention will be on praising God and not be diverted to the evil one. Let's strive to keep everyone's focus on Jesus.

Defeated Enemy

Satan's divine appointment with Jesus is coming soon. The chosen generation and royal priesthood's enemy knows he has a meeting that he cannot cancel. Because on that day, he must bow his knees and confess with his mouth that Jesus Christ is Lord.

Regarding Jesus, it is written,

> And being found in appearance as a man, He humbled Himself and became obedient to *the point of* death, even the death of the cross. Therefore God also has highly exalted Him and given Him the name which is above every name, that at the name of Jesus every knee should bow, of those in heaven, and of those on earth, and of those under the . . .

> . . . earth, and *that* every tongue should confess that Jesus Christ *is* Lord, to the glory of God the Father. —Philippians 2:8–11 (NKJV)

I like to fantasize about when Jesus will be seated on His throne in all of His glory. Embarrassed, Satan will cower before King Jesus, squirm from one bended knee to another, and choke out his most dreaded words, JESUS is LORD, before God and His saints.

> Therefore I also, after I heard of your faith in the Lord Jesus and your love for all the saints, do not cease to give thanks for you, making mention of you in my prayers: that the God of our Lord Jesus Christ, the Father of glory, may give to you the spirit of wisdom and revelation in the knowledge of Him, the eyes of your understanding being enlightened; that you may know what is the hope of His calling, what are the riches of the glory of His inheritance in the saints, and what *is* the exceeding greatness of His power toward us who believe, according to the working of His mighty power which He worked in Christ when He raised Him from the dead and seated *Him* at His right hand in the heavenly *places,* far above all principality and power and might and dominion, and every name that is named, not only in this age but also in that which is to come. . . .

Choices & Strongholds

— By Mary A. Bruno, Ph.D.

> . . . And He put all *things* under His feet, and gave Him *to be* head over all *things* to the church, which is His body, the fullness of Him who fills all in all. —Ephesians 1:15–23 (NKJV)

> For our wrestling is not against flesh and blood, but against the principalities, against the powers, against the world-rulers of this darkness, against the spiritual *hosts* of wickedness in the heavenly *places*. —Ephesians 6:12 (ASV)

Still Kicking, But Not For Long!

During my childhood, we girls (four of us) watched when my father butchered chickens. Those rowdy birds were strange creatures. Even with their heads chopped-off, they still darted all over the yard and scared us out of our wits.

The chickens were dead—but their nerves didn't know it. We knew they were dead—but were terrified of their flapping wings and flopping feet.

Daddy grabbed the darting dead chickens, threw them in a sack, and stopped their scary sideshow.

In the Bag!

By now, you are getting the idea; the devil is a lot like those finished floppy feathered fowl. He knows he is finished, but still darts about and kicks up a lot of dust. All we need to do is to bind him (bag him) in Jesus's name. He cannot harm us, but if we leave him alone, he will continue to run amok, put on a good show, and stir up dirt, fear, and trouble.

The enemy still works through powers; principalities (ruling entities over geographical locations and within geographic boundaries), and through spiritual wickedness in high places during this age. Nevertheless, the evil one's strength and abilities are limited, and his time is rapidly running out.

Our Sparring Partner

We must keep in mind that Jesus gave us power over all of Satan's power. Not just some of it. Jesus expects us to do what He authorized us to do and not come crying for Him to do it for us.

> Behold, I have given you authority to tread upon serpents and scorpions, and over all the power of the enemy: and nothing shall in any wise hurt you. —Luke 10:19 (ASV)

Jesus gave us a voice-trained enemy that must obey us. However, it is our responsibility to issue the commands.

Jesus, Captain of our Salvation, left a defeated enemy around to keep us in shape and from getting spiritually flabby. He left His defeated enemy, for us to use as a sparring partner for military exercises, while we learn to perfect our warring skills and prepare to pass our tests.

> Now these *are* the nations which the LORD left, that He might test Israel by them, *that is,* all who had not known any of the wars in Canaan (*this was* only so that the generations of the children of Israel might be taught to know war, at least those who had not formerly known it), *namely, five lords of the Philistines,* all the Canaanites, the Sidonians, and the Hivites who dwelt in Mount Lebanon, from Mount Baal Hermon to the entrance of Hamath.
> — Judges 3:1– 3 (NKJV)
> Emphasis added.

Since the *five lords of the Philistines* are mentioned, let's dig a little deeper to find what they represent. The word *lords,* means *tyrants*. The five *lords* were five *Philistine tyrants* who were Israel's enemies. The *tyrants* ruled over the following five cities:

1. Gaza: (H5804)

"the strong," "fortified"

2. Ashkelon (H831)

"a weighing place"

3. Ashdod (H795

"powerful", " a fortified place", from a word that means, *"ravager"*

4. Ekron (H6138)

"emigration" or *"torn up by the roots,"* from a word meaning *"eradication"*

5. Gath (H1661)

"winepress" or *"trough"* where grapes were trodden with the feet. The place where the giant, Goliath, was born.

> And they were *left that He might* test Israel by them, to know whether they would obey the commandments of the LORD, which He had commanded their fathers by the hand of Moses.
> — Judges 3:4 (NKJV)

God has equipped and authorized us to overcome all that comes against us. We must not laze around, but must know when it is time to put our spiritual skills and authority into action, dare to obey God, take down tyrants, pull down strongholds, and then build and plant for God's glory.

Comments:

_____

_____

_____

_____

_____

_____

***

Choices & Strongholds

— By Mary A. Bruno, Ph.D.

> And the children of Israel again did evil in the sight of the LORD. So the LORD strengthened Eglon king of Moab against Israel, because they had done evil in the sight of the LORD.
> —Judges 3:12 (NKJV)

> So the children of Israel served Eglon king of Moab eighteen years.
>
> But when the children of Israel cried out to the LORD, the LORD raised up a deliverer for them: Ehud the son of Gera, the Benjamite, a left-handed man. By him the children of Israel sent tribute to Eglon king of Moab.
> —Judges 3:14–15 (NKJV)

10
Do Something

Judges, Chapter three tells of Ehud's exciting, courageous, and inventive story. His adventure opens with what happened when the Israelites not only, forgot to obey the LORD, but they did evil in the sight of the LORD, and became entrapped in a stronghold.

Things went from bad to worse. They were in bondage under King Eglon, had served him for 18 years, and in a miserable mess, when somebody realized it was time to cry out to God for help.

Their lives were in a sad state, but it was not too late. Let's see what God did when His people remembered to pray.

Make an Effort and Use Your Weapon

God raised up Ehud to stop King Eglon's oppression. Ehud made a two-edged dagger, which reminds us of God's two-edged sword. Ehud hand-delivered his gift to the King.

> So Ehud came to him (now he was sitting upstairs in his cool private chamber). Then Ehud said, "I have a message from God for you." So he arose from *his* seat. Then Ehud reached with his left hand, took the dagger from his right thigh, and thrust it into his belly. Even the hilt went in after the blade, and the fat closed over the blade, for he did not draw the dagger out of his belly; and his entrails came out.
> —Judges 3:20–22 (NKJV)

Ehud's obedience put an end to the tyranny and brought freedom to the Israelites. Like Ehud with Eglon, let's dare to use the Sword of the Spirit to destroy demonic dominions and set loved ones free. Let's not hold back, but thrust that Sword of the Spirit in to the hilt!

Choices & Strongholds

— By Mary A. Bruno, Ph.D.

Root Out, Resist, and Confront

Like Jeremiah, let's: root out; let's pull down; let's throw down; let's destroy the works of the evil one; and then, let's build and plant for God. We have read some of these verses before, but let's reread them—because they are so good!

> For though we walk in the flesh, we do not war according to the flesh. For the weapons of our warfare *are* not carnal but mighty in God for pulling down strongholds, casting down arguments and every high thing that exalts itself against the knowledge of God, bringing every thought into captivity to the obedience of Christ,
> —2 Corinthians 10:3–5 (NKJV)

Like the early church, let's pull down strongholds; let's cast down imaginations; and let's bring every thought and strategy into captivity and obedience to Jesus Christ.

> Submit yourselves therefore to God. Resist the devil, and he will flee from you.   —James 4:7 (KJV)

Let's resist the devil and watch him flee from us.

> "Assuredly, I say to you, whatever you bind on earth will be bound in heaven, and whatever you loose on earth will be loosed in heaven."
> —Matthew 18:18 (NKJV)

Jesus is waiting for us to act in His name. Let's bind on earth what God has bound in Heaven.

> So Jesus answered and said to them, "Assuredly, I say to you, if you have faith and do not doubt, you will not only do what was done to the fig tree, but also if you say to this mountain, 'Be removed and be cast into the sea,' it will be done.'"
> —Matthew 21:21 (NKJV)

> So the Lord said, "If you have faith as a mustard seed, you can say to this mulberry tree, 'Be pulled up by the roots and be planted in the sea,' and it would obey you.'"
> —Luke 17:6 (NKJV)

Let's confront and command unfruitful trees (growths) to "Move!" Let's uproot our family trees of unrighteousness and send them where they cannot survive. Let's confront our obedience-trained enemy, order him out of our lives, and cast his influence out of our bloodlines.

> "Heal the sick, cleanse the lepers, raise the dead, cast out demons. Freely you have received, freely give.'"
> —Matthew 10:8 (NKJV)

Let's dare to heal the sick; dare to cleanse the lepers; dare to raise the dead, and dare to cast out demons. Let's dare to freely receive and dare to freely give.

> So Jesus said to them again, "Peace to you! As the Father has sent Me, I also send you."
> —John 20:21 (NKJV)

Our fully-equipped Jesus has sent His fully-equipped followers to go in His name. Let's muster our courage and take some action, in Jesus's mighty name!

Intercede

Amazing things happen when parents pray for their children. Demons must leave when parents intercede. St. Matthew wrote about a mother's appeal to Jesus on behalf of her *severely demonized* daughter. The woman was irritating and a lot like we read about blind Bartimaeus in Chapter one.

> And behold, a woman of Canaan came from that region and cried out to Him, saying, "Have mercy on me, O Lord, Son of David! My daughter is severely demon-possessed." But He answered her not a word.
> And His disciples came and urged Him, saying, "Send her away, for she cries out after us."
> But He answered and said, "I was not sent except to the lost sheep of the house of Israel."
> Then she came and worshiped Him, saying, "Lord, help me!"
> But He answered and said, "It is not good to take the children's bread and throw *it* to the little dogs." . . .

> . . . And she said, "Yes, Lord, yet even the little dogs eat the crumbs which fall from their masters' table." Then Jesus answered and said to her, "O woman, great *is* your faith! Let it be to you as you desire." And her daughter was healed from that very hour. —Matthew 15:22–28 (NKJV)

Note! The daughter was absent, and there was no hint that she agreed with her mother's plea for her deliverance. This passage sets a precedent for parents to intercede for their children. At times youngsters, teenagers, or adult children, get so out of hand when under demonic influence, they cannot use good judgment. But, when even one parent prays for them and trusts Jesus will set them free, that parent can have what he or she asks. The children's bread includes deliverance and healing.

Diseases and Demons Obeyed

When New Testament believers brought handkerchiefs or aprons from Paul to the sick, *diseases departed*, and *evil spirits left*.

> And God wrought special miracles by the hands of Paul: insomuch that unto the sick were carried away from his body handkerchiefs or aprons, and the diseases departed from them, and the evil spirits went out.
> —Acts 19:11–12 (ASV)

There must have been *usual* miracles in addition to the *unusual* miracles. How nice!

> And he stood over her, and rebuked the fever; and it left her: and immediately she rose up and ministered unto them.
> —Luke 4:39 (ASV)

Did you notice diseases and fevers had the ability to get up and leave? They must obey when God's people act in faith. Anything that can be rebuked has the capacity to understand. It must submit to your God-given authority and command. So, do not stand there staring. Jesus expects you to exercise your rights and order the unclean spirit, sickness, virus, or disease to leave!

Your Marriage and Your Flesh

> And He answered and said to them, "Have you not read that He who made *them* at the beginning 'made them male and female,' and said, 'For this reason a man shall leave his father and mother and be joined to his wife, and the two shall become one flesh'?
> So then, they are no longer two but one flesh. Therefore what God has joined together, let not man separate." —Matthew 19:4–6 (NKJV)

Because a married couple has become one flesh, the husband and the wife each have a voice in what goes on in his or her spouse's flesh.

The enemy may try to trick us into thinking otherwise, "Because the other person has his or her free will." However, God's Word assures we do have authority in the matter—because the husband's flesh is the wife's flesh, and the wife's flesh has become one with her husband. Therefore, each can watch over and exercise their authority in Christ to protect the other from evil flesh-traps and schemes.

> "Assuredly, I say to you, whatever you bind on earth will be bound in heaven, and whatever you loose on earth will be loosed in heaven."
> —Matthew 18:18 (NKJV)

Whenever a husband or wife finds enemy tactics at work in his or her spouse, it is time to exercise his or her God-given right to bind (forbid) that ungodly activity in Jesus's name and order it to stop.

The Blood Line

Old Testament priests applied animal blood to cover sin. The chosen generation and royal priesthood proclaim the power of Jesus's Holy, Divine Blood, to set boundaries and limitations that stop powers and principalities that have influenced our mates and families for generations.

Choices & Strongholds

— By Mary A. Bruno, Ph.D.

> Therefore submit to God. Resist the devil and he will flee from you. Draw near to God and He will draw near to you.
> —James 4:7–8a (NKJV)

Comments:

_____

_____

_____

_____

_____

_____

_____

When we resist the enemy, he flees from (shuns) us. When we come closer to God; He comes closer to us.

Expect Jesus to start showing up more often as you come closer to Him.

Next, we shall address voluntary and involuntary strongholds.

＊＊＊

> *"There is* an accursed thing in your midst,
> O Israel; you cannot stand before your enemies until you take away the accursed thing from among you." —Joshua 7:13B (NKJV)

11
Stronghold Indicators

I pause to acknowledge and thank Jimmy Maynor, for his excellent work in his two-page article entitled [27]"Pulling Down Strongholds." His work greatly enriched the study on this subject and inspired much of the following.

Involuntary and Voluntary Strongholds

Involuntary strongholds may have developed from childhood. They might have resulted from lies we heard about ourselves (negative talk) or the dark powers we or our relatives entertained.

Strongholds can grow from things one has chosen or welcomed by making room for them in his or her life: fear; anger; violence; perversions, addictions, etcetera.

Achan's Family

Many have heard about when Joshua took the city of Jericho.

Everyone had clear directions regarding what to do or not to do during that victory.

> "Now the city shall be doomed by the LORD to destruction, it and all who *are* in it. Only Rahab the harlot shall live, she and all who *are* with her in the house, because she hid the messengers that we sent. And you, by all means abstain from the accursed things, lest you become accursed when you take of the accursed things, and make the camp of Israel a curse, and trouble it. But all the silver and gold, and vessels of bronze and iron, *are* consecrated to the LORD; they shall come into the treasury of the LORD." —Joshua 6:17–19 (NKJV)

We must be aware that the enemy may show up during our most significant moments of victory and attack us where we are most vulnerable during our overconfident and off-guard moments.

Achan's sin of greed and his love of forbidden things mushroomed into a cursed stronghold of lust and desire that not only, doomed him, but his entire family, and stole victory from the whole camp.

> But the children of Israel committed a trespass regarding the accursed things, for Achan the son of Carmi, the son of Zabdi, the son of Zerah, of the tribe of Judah, took of the . . .

> . . . accursed things; so the anger of the LORD burned against the children of Israel. —Joshua 7:1 (NKJV)

Tip! We should avoid doing anything that will invite God's anger to seethe against us.

One family member's hidden sin impacted his whole household. Achan's sin not only affected each family member, but the entire camp lost God's blessing. Joshua's, once brave, soldiers ran in fear for their lives and could not stand before the men of the small town of Ai while the accursed things' coverup continued.

God told Joshua how to resolve the problem, which took courage to confront. It would not be pretty but had to be done.

> Therefore the children of Israel could not stand before their enemies, *but* turned *their* backs before their enemies, because they have become doomed to destruction. Neither will I be with you anymore, unless you destroy the accursed from among you. —Joshua 7:12 (NKJV)

Again, we read of how hidden sin brought defeat.

> "*There is* an accursed thing in your midst, O Israel; you cannot stand before your enemies until you take away the accursed thing from among you." —Joshua 7:13b (NKJV)

Be wise and do not go out to fight against an enemy with hidden sin in your tent or while you are covering up for someone else's ongoing sin.

Achan's confession seemed like a replay of Eve's declaration of guilt in Genesis Chapter three.

Although deceived, Eve chose to rebel against God and brought sin's curse on the Human Race when she saw; she coveted; she took, and she hid. She could trace her sin-steps but could not undo the damage she had done to herself and others.

> And Achan answered Joshua and said, "Indeed I have sinned against the LORD God of Israel, and this is what I have done: When I saw among the spoils a beautiful Babylonian garment, two hundred shekels of silver, and a wedge of gold weighing fifty shekels, I coveted them and took them. And there they are, hidden in the earth in the midst of my tent, with the silver under it." —Joshua 7:20–21 (NKJV)

Achan was fully informed —but not deceived— when he saw, he coveted, he took, he hid, and he brought sin's consequences on his loved ones. The silver and gold that he stole belonged to God! (The wedge of gold weighing 50 shekels weighed about 20 ounces.) Taking them was the equivalent of stealing God's tithe and offerings—which involved a curse.

Choices & Strongholds — By Mary A. Bruno, Ph.D.

> "Will a man rob God?
> Yet you have robbed Me!
> But you say,
> 'In what way have we robbed You?'
> In tithes and offerings.
> You are cursed with a curse,
> For you have robbed Me,
> *Even* this whole nation."
> —Malachi 3:8–9 (NKJV)

Hidden Sin Affects the Whole Family

As we know, Achan's hush-hushed sin brought heartbreak and disaster to his nearest and dearest. *They* suffered the anguish of stoning because of *his* hidden sin. Covering *his* ears could not stop *their* screams or the horror of seeing his wife and children being stoned and burned when judgment fell upon them all.

Achan's secret sin drew an open and harsh reward. He may have shown the loot to his family before hiding it in their tent. They may have known about it but kept the matter quiet. Whether aware or unaware of his theft of what belonged to God, the entire family suffered and lost their lives because of one rebel's greed and rebellion.

Hidden Sin Affects the Whole Camp

The judgment did not stop with Achan's family. The whole camp was defeated and could not prosper while secret sin was among them.

Thirty-six brave warriors died when they went to battle against Ai.

Fear sapped the soldiers' courage. They could not prevail against their enemies while a sinful cover-up was in the camp.

When God's blessings depart—check the heart. Sin might be hiding in your camp.

How Strongholds Develop

Strongholds can develop in different ways, including the following:

Entertain/ Contemplate/Yield

A stronghold may begin when a person is attracted, nibbles at the bait, starts to entertain a thought, and dwells on it. He or she may go out to play with the devil, flirt with his wiles, and toy with the possibility of allowing an ungodly action or forbidden thing. One may study it and try to find a way to fit it into one's life.

A stronghold settles in when one embraces a favorable attitude toward an action or deed. He or she entertains, sides with the idea, agrees with it, and tries to justify the behavior. He or she defends it and twists Scripture out of context to support his or her warped views and carnal cravings.

A stronghold formation is evident when a person repeatedly resists God and yields to the desire. The action that was intended "*Just for this one time*", forms a *hook* in one's mind or flesh that gets repeated, as a sin habit takes hold.

Choices & Strongholds   — By Mary A. Bruno, Ph.D.

Soon, the person becomes addicted to the sin. It fills his or her thoughts, replays again and again, and demands more. He or she plans for the next time and place to do it again, which confirms the *hook* is deeply embedded.

What began as a *one-time-only* stolen moment of indulgence, or pleasure, seizes him or her like the steel jaws of a trap. He or she struggles to get free and panics, knowing he or she is trapped. What began as pleasure is no longer fun.

Captivity and Torment

The stronghold is in control when a time and place are reserved to repeat the act. The person wants to quit, but it is too late. The entangled person struggles but cannot break free.

Thankfully, our Loving Father God knows how and is very good at turning our impossibilities into possibilities. Call on Him; take His advice, and see what happens.

When the demon is sure he has captured his prey, he moves in, like a cat to toy with a mouse before the kill. He batters the mind with accusations and strikes with blows of torment, contempt, ridicule, depression, self-loathing, self-condemnation, and fear of exposure. Being caught in a stronghold is a bitter, hurting, and humbling experience, but God's power can break it.

How to Recognize Strongholds

When a person regularly confesses the same matter to God, and daily asks to be set free, a stronghold may be involved. He or she promises never to do it again but fails repeatedly, which brings more self-disgust and self-condemnation.

The trapped person cannot understand why he or she keeps repeating the sin and wonders why he or she is so weak. The habit hangs on like a relentless biting monkey on his or her back.

Habitual Excess

Any area of repeated or habitual excess in one's life may indicate a stronghold. A person may hide it for fear of exposure and wrestles with shame and embarrassment. The victim fears disclosure could ruin relationships with his loved ones, friends, ministry, church, and employer.

The hooked or ensnared person may withdraw from God—which is the absolute last thing that should ever happen. He or she is too ashamed to go to Jesus about it, but Jesus is the only way to victory and freedom. He or she prays, but nothing changes.

Why?

It is because he or she is trapped in a stronghold. One does not pray oneself out of a stronghold. He or she must exercise his or her rights in Christ and dare to *confront* and *command* his or her way out.

Comments:

_____

_____

_____

_____

_____

_____

_____

_____

_____

***

---

[27] Jimmy Maynor, <u>The Witness</u>, "Pulling Down Strongholds"; Vol III, No.2; March, 1983.

> Behold, I give you the authority to trample on serpents and scorpions, and over all the power of the enemy, and nothing shall by any means hurt you.   —Luke 10:19 (NKJV)

12
Demolish Strongholds

At this point, it is time to pull down the stronghold. As Jimmy Maynard mentioned in his *Pulling Down* Strongholds[28] article, we can repent and confess, and repent and confess, until we are exhausted, but confession will not break a stronghold.

Repentance and confession bring God's forgiveness, but, another step is needed before the person can be free. He or she must *confront* his or her stronghold!

Be Firm

Years ago, we had a big outside dog—a Collie named Sally. Sally knew she was supposed to stay in the yard, but now and then, she would sneak into the house. On one such occasion, the freshly polished floor was still wet, when in crept Sally. I yelled, from across the room, and barked a command for that sneaky dog to *Get out of there!*

Sally spun around with toenails clicking against the floor, and bolted out as if her tail were on fire!

Sometimes, the enemy is like Sally; he knows he does not belong in a person's life, but will wait around and sneak in if someone leaves the door open. If he gets in, he will try to hide until someone confronts him and orders him out. When caught in the act and ordered out, he knows he must give up and will flee.

Be Bold

Facing the problem is necessary. A person can dance around and side-step it all he or she pleases, and hope it will leave. But sometime, somewhere, he or she is going to have to take a stand against it, side with Jesus, exercise his or her authority in Christ, and *order* the unclean spirit to go.

There is no need to be afraid of our voiced-trained enemy. He is afraid of us and hopes we will not speak up. Thank God for our spiritual weapons in 2 Corinthians 10:3–5. Let's use them!

Even a child can exercise God-given authority in Christ. One of my daughters was in the third or fourth grade when she and a friend got off their school bus. A large savage-looking dog saw them from across the street, bared his fangs, barked, growled, and ran toward them in a terrifying attack mode.

Knowing her privileges in Christ, she looked that dog straight in the eye, stretched forth her dainty little hand, and commanded, *"I rebuke you in Jesus's name!"*

The dog halted as if shot! He shut his mouth, lowered his head, turned around, and cowered back across the street with his tail between his legs.

"Wow!" her friend said, "How did you do that?"

"There is power in the name of Jesus," my daughter explained.

The encounter might have ended differently if she had not dared to rebuke the attacker in front of her friend. But, when she spoke that rebuke in Jesus's name, He took immediate action and enforced her order.

Pluck it up by the Root

As believers, we need to root out wrong thinking. We need to agree with God. We must take every thought captive and insist they submit to and obey Christ. We must surrender ourselves to God, stop playing with the enemy, and *resist* the devil.

We must be sure we are indeed born again, then identify the strongholds and pull them down from our lives and the lives of others. The chosen generation and royal priesthood are authorized and able to demolish strongholds, wherever they appear. Just because one has never done it before does not mean that he, she, or you cannot start now.

Search and Destroy.

The following steps may be helpful when God's servants dare to confront and destroy strongholds: We can identify a stronghold (a spiritual fortress), know when or how it started, call it by name, bind its power, and order it to leave.

Start at the Beginning

Trace it back to the first time.

Where was the person?

Who else was there?

What was he or she wearing?

What was he or she eating?

What was he or she smoking?

What was he or she snorting?

What was he or she drinking?

What was he or she reading?

What was he or she viewing?

What was he or she touching?

What was he or she discussing?

To whom or to what was he or she listening?

Identify who or what opened the door to the sin or compromise that became a stronghold, then close that point of entry— permanently!

Break Fellowship with the Stronghold

Encourage the person (or yourself) to give it up and break it off. Tell the one who is bound that he or she (or you) must submit to God and resist [turn against] the devil and his pleasures [strongholds] to get completely free.

Break up with it! Tell it not to come back! Fill your mind with God's Word. Change your daily habits to include time for prayer, praise, godly friends, and church.

Behave as though the Work is Done

Encourage the person to:

1. Believe the work is done. Start behaving as though he or she is (or you are) free of the stronghold.

2. Teach the person to praise and thank God for victory and freedom.

3. Encourage that one, or yourself, to stay away from the people who, or things that, tried to lure him or her, or you, away from God.

4. Advise to keep out of the old places and traps and act as if he or she is, or you are, free.

5. Dare to trample on that which used to trample on you.

> Behold, I give you the authority to trample on serpents and scorpions, and over all the power of the enemy, and nothing shall by any means hurt you. —Luke 10:19 (NKJV)

Always remember that Jesus has entrusted us with His power that is over *all* of the enemy's ability (wherever we find it working). We must not only know about it—but we must dare to use the authority that Jesus gave to us. In His name, we must get free, stay free, and set others free.

> Therefore if the Son makes you free, you shall be free indeed.
> —John 8:36 (NKJV)

Clean Up and Clean Out Your Home

Principalities may have entered or may be operating in your home through ungodly things:

1. Videos and movies

2. Books and magazines

3. Cultic literature and materials (Ouija boards, magic, witchcraft, pornography, etc.)

4. Idols, charms (objects associated with Halloween decorations, witch-craft, heathen worship), etc.

5. Ill-gotten gain, (gifts, garments or property from unholy associations, or stolen property)

6. Ungodly music

7. Addictive substances.

> And not a few of them that practised magical arts brought their books together and burned them in the sight of all; and they counted the price of them, and found it fifty thousand pieces of silver.
> — Acts 19:19 (ASV)

If in doubt, throw them out and bind the principalities working behind or through them.

Associations

Principalities; influence through associations. Avoid being around those who weigh you down spiritually, such as:

1. Rebels

2. Gossips

3. People caught up in gratifying the lusts of their flesh, including alcohol, drugs, gambling, and other addictions

4. Practicing addicts

5. Practicing criminals

Beware of that which flatters the flesh, steals the heart, and binds the soul.

Other Areas

Bind and cast out principalities at work in other areas, such as:

1. Immorality: incest, rape, prostitution, fornication [sexual intercourse between unmarried people], adultery (sexual intercourse between a married person and someone to whom he or she is not married), perversion, pornography, other sexual sins that God's Word forbids.

2. Violence: family abuse (physical, emotional or verbal abuse), murder, crime, vice, theft, robbery, unforgiveness, greed.

3. Addictions: alcoholism, narcotics, food, other substances, gambling, gaming, video games, pornography, shoplifting, etc.

4. False doctrine: idolatry, occult teachings, witchcraft, voodoo, Satan worship, fortunetelling, divination, astrology, lying, prejudice, or excess.

5. Diseases and illness

Human kind's body and blood may have given one a dreaded disease, but Jesus Christ's body and blood can take it away.

The Bad News

> Do you not know that the unrighteous will not inherit the kingdom of God? Do not be deceived. Neither fornicators, nor idolaters, nor adulterers, nor homosexuals, or Sodomites, nor thieves, nor covetous, nor drunkards, nor revilers, nor extortioners will inherit the kingdom of God.
> —1 Corinthians 6:9–10 (NKJV)

The Good News

> And such were some of you. But you were washed, but you were sanctified, but you were justified in the name of the Lord Jesus and by the Spirit of our God.
> —1 Corinthians 6:11 (NKJV)

Comments:

_____

_____

_____

_____

Choices & Strongholds

— By Mary A. Bruno, Ph.D.

Want to Write a Review?

1. If you have *purchased* this book, entitled, *Choices & Strongholds* by Mary A. Bruno, Ph.D., from Amazon.com and found that reading it was helpful, please take a moment to write a review on www.amazon.com. She reads them all.

2. If this book was *a gift to you* or purchased directly from Dr. Bruno, and you wish to write a review, please email your comments directly to her at imibcs@aol.com. You may also send them by regular mail to:

> Mary A. Bruno, Ph.D.
> P.O. Box 2107
> Vista, CA 92085-2107
> United States of America

How to write a review on www.Amazon.com —It's easy!

1. Type, www.amazon.com, on your web browser.
2. Type, *Mary A. Bruno, Ph.D.,* (Case sensitive) on Amazon's search bar, and then click on the magnifying glass.
3. Click on the book's title: *Choices & Strongholds!*
4. Click on the *customer reviews* (blue writing), by the yellow rating stars (next to a picture of the book).
5. Read a few reviews, if there are any, to get an idea of what goes into one, or skip this step and write your review.
6. Click on the (gray) *Write a Customer Review* box, and then complete the *Sign In* box that pops up.
7. Dare to wax eloquent and compose a review with your unique observations and style. Thank you!

Bibliography

Resources consulted during research for this book, entitled *Choices & Strongholds,* include the following:

Books

American Standard Version (ASV)
Public Domain

Amplified Bible (AMP)
Copyright © 2015 by The Lockman Foundation, La Habra, CA 90631. All rights reserved.

The Chicago Manual of Style, Sixteenth Edition.
Chicago: The University of Chicago Press, 2010.

Jubilee Bible 2000 (JUB)
Copyright © 2013, 2020 by Ransom Press International

New King James Version (NKJV)
Scripture taken from the New King James Version®. Copyright © 1982 by Thomas Nelson. Used by permission. All rights reserved.

The New Strong's Exhaustive Concordance of the Bible
Strong, James, LL.D., S.T.D. Nashville, Thomas Nelson Publishers, 1990

The Pentateuch; Holdcroft, Thomas L.; Western Book Company; Oakland, California; 1966

The Witness; Vol III, No 2; "Pulling Down Strongholds"; Jimmy Maynor; (address unknown); March 1983.\

Webster's New Collegiate Dictionary, G. & C. Merriam Company, Springfield, MA, 1975

Websites Contacted

BibleGateway
https://www.biblegateway.com/

BlueLetterBible.org
https://www.blueletterbible.org

THE END (Book Two)

[28] Jimmy Maynor, The Witness, "Pulling Down Strongholds"; Vol III, No.2; March 1983.

STUDY GUIDE/ JOURNAL —FOR USE WITH— Why Shofars Wail in Scripture and Today —The Exciting Stories and Miracles!

Authored by Mary A. Bruno, Ph.D.

Ideal for Individual Study or Groups!

ISBN: 9780997668155

Want to learn more from your shofar study?

Discover God's long-range plans for shofar blowers and people affected by their ministry.

Understand how God prepared and helped them and still helps folks today.

Recognize God's guidance that led to where you are now.

New to guided study and journaling? This is an excellent way to begin. God will illuminate places in His Word that will flood your soul with the precious truth that begs to go into your journal. Those sacred *nuggets*/journal entries will become love gifts from God and treasured wisdom for reflection and teaching that are ideal for personal or group study and spiritual enrichment!

"Like us," Ministry Lit, on Facebook!

Order Today!
ISBN: 9780997668155
~~$17.99~~ **$14.99** US Dollars plus tax, S&H in the Continental. U.S.

Dr. Bruno's unsigned books are available at www.amazon.com. (Just type: Mary A. Bruno, Ph.D. on Amazon's search bar and her book titles should appear.)

To request autographed copies of Dr. Bruno's writings,

Email: imibcs@aol.com

Or write:
Mary A. Bruno, Ph.D.
P.O. Box 2107
Vista, California 92085-2107
United States of America

How to Order this Book

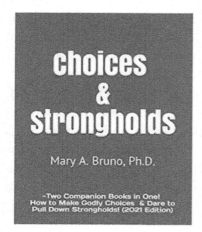

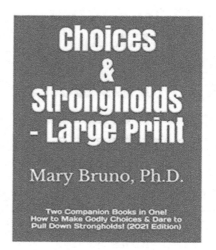

ISBN: 9780997668124

How to avoid traps, make godly choices, and set goals that lead to a blessed life of joy, peace, love, ministry, and prosperity.

Tired of losing battles with a besetting sin? Learn who you are in Christ and Who Christ is in you!

Rise up in holy boldness! Use your God-given authority and spiritual weapons to crush strongholds!

Become the champion God has ordained you to be!

Put principalities on the run!
Walk in victory!
Take new territory for Christ!
Easy to Read!
Great for bilingual booklovers.

Order Today!
ISBN: 9780997668124

$10.99 U.S. Dollars plus tax, S&H in the Continental U.S.
Buy one for yourself and a friend.

ISBN: 9780997668131

Order Today!
ISBN: 9780997668131
$12.99 (Large Print) U.S. Dollars plus tax, S&H in Continental U.S.

> The Large Print version has this size type.

Dr. Bruno's unsigned books are available at www.amazon.com. (Just type *Mary A. Bruno, Ph.D.* on Amazon's search bar and her book titles should appear.)

To request autographed copies of Dr. Bruno's writings,
Email: imibcs@aol.com
Or write:
Mary A. Bruno, Ph.D.
P.O. Box 2107
Vista, California 92085-2107
United States of America

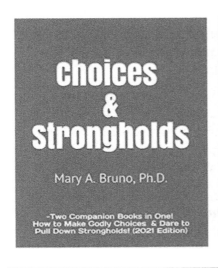

How to Donate
Choices & Strongholds

Adults and teens in jails, prisons, juvenile halls, or recovery homes, and our heroic veterans, need God's help and guidance.

Your gift can change lives.

Make check or money order payable to:
Interdenominational Ministries International (IMI)

Mail to
Interdenominational Ministries International (IMI)
P.O. Box 2107
Vista, California 92085-2107
United States of America

IMI is a Tax-Exempt 501(C)(3) Non-profit Organization.
Your entire gift marked *"Books"* will be used solely to donate these books.

How to share your testimony of how God has helped you.

A form is provided at the end of this book. If it is missing, Dr. Bruno and others will still be encouraged by reading how God has helped you and made a difference in your life. You are invited use the following guideline to help tell how the Lord Jesus has made a difference in your life. Then, please sign, date, and mail it to:

Interdenominational Ministries International (IMI)
P.O. Box 2107
Vista, CA 90285-2107
United States of America

1. Tell what your life was like before you read this book.

2. Tell what changed since you learned more about Jesus.

3. Tell what your life is like now.

4. Add any other comments.

5. Please, copy one of the following statements to give IMI permission to share or to not share your testimony:

Yes, _____ You may share my testimony in print or by electronic means, including the internet, etc., for God's glory and to encourage others.

No, ____ Please, do not share my testimony.

Please print.

Name:

Age:

The Date:

Sign your name.

Print your

Address:

City

State

Zip Code

Email:

COMBO-VCS-2021Ed-172--7.5X9.25-170P-042521

If God has used this book to help you...

Dr. Bruno and others will be encouraged by reading how God has helped you. You are invited to write your brief **testimony of how the Lord Jesus has made a difference in your life**, and then sign, date, and mail this completed form to:
Interdenominational Ministries International (IMI)
P.O. Box 2107
Vista, CA 90285-2107 United States of America

_____
_____
_____
_____
_____
_____
_____
_____
_____
_____
_____
_____
_____
_____

_____
_____
_____
_____
_____
_____
_____
_____
_____
_____
_____
_____
_____
_____
_____
_____
_____

(Continue on side two if more space is needed.)

Please, check one:
Yes, _____You may share my testimony in print or by electronic means, including the internet, etc., for God's glory and to encourage others.
No, _____Please, do not share my testimony.

Please print your name._____

_____

Age: _____Date:_____
Signature: _____
Address: _____
City _____
State_____
Zip Code _____
Email _____

CO COMBO-VCS-2021Ed-172--7.5X9.25-170P-042521

If God has used this book to help you...

Dr. Bruno and others will be encouraged by reading how God has helped you. You are invited to write your brief **testimony of how the Lord Jesus has made a difference in your life**, and then sign, date, and mail this completed form to:

Interdenominational Ministries International (IMI)
P.O. Box 2107
Vista, CA 90285-2107 United States of America

_____

_____

_____

_____

_____

_____

_____

_____

_____

_____

_____

_____

_____

_____

_____

_____

_____

_____

_____

_____

_____

_____

_____

_____

_____

_____

_____

_____

_____

_____

_____

_____

(Continue on side two if more space is needed.)

Please, check one:

Yes, _____ **You may share my testimony** in print or by electronic means, including the internet, etc., for God's glory and to encourage others.

No, _____ **Please, do not share my testimony.**

Please print your name._____

_____

Age: _____ Date:_____

Signature: _____

Address: _____

City _____

State_____

Zip Code _____

Email _____

COMBO-VCS-2021Ed-172-7.5X9.25-170P-042521

Choices & Stronghold   — By Mary A. Bruno, Ph.D.

Made in the USA
Middletown, DE
19 June 2022

67316057R00097